ΔD Architectural Design

Back To School: Architectural Education – the Information and the Argument

Guest-edited by Michael Chadwick

⟨w⟩WILEY-ACADEMY

Architectural Design
Vol 74 No 5 Sept/Oct 2004

ISBN 0470870753

Profile No 171

Editorial Offices
International House
Ealing Broadway Centre
London W5 5DB
T: +44 (0)20 8326 3800
F: +44 (0)20 8326 3801
E: architecturaldesign@wiley.co.uk

Editor
Helen Castle

Production
Mariangela Palazzi-Williams

Art Direction/Design
Christian Küsters (CHK Design)

Design Assistant
Hannah Dumphy (CHK Design)

**Project Coordinator
and Picture Editor**
Caroline Ellerby

Advertisement Sales
01243 843272

Editorial Board
Denise Bratton, Adriaan Beukers,
André Chaszar, Peter Cook,
Max Fordham, Massimiliano
Fuksas, Edwin Heathcote,
Anthony Hunt, Charles Jencks,
Jan Kaplicky, Robert Maxwell,
Jayne Merkel, Monica Pidgeon,
Antoine Predock, Leon van Schaik

Contributing Editors
André Chaszar
Craig Kellogg
Jeremy Melvin
Jayne Merkel

Subscription Offices UK
John Wiley & Sons Ltd.
Journals Administration Department
1 Oldlands Way, Bognor Regis
West Sussex, PO22 9SA
T: +44 (0)1243 843272
F: +44 (0)1243 843232
E: cs-journals@wiley.co.uk

Annual Subscription Rates 2004
Institutional Rate: UK £175
Personal Rate: UK £99
Student Rate: UK £70
Institutional Rate: US $270
Personal Rate: US $155
Student Rate: US $110
ᴧᴅ is published bi-monthly.
Prices are for six issues and include
postage and handling charges.
Periodicals postage paid at Jamaica,
NY 11431. Air freight and mailing
in the USA by Publications
Expediting Services Inc, 200 Meacham
Avenue, Elmont, NY 11003

Single Issues UK: £22.50
Single Issues outside UK: US $45.00
Details of postage and packing charges
available on request

Postmaster
Send address changes to ᴧᴅ Publications
Expediting Services, 200 Meacham Avenue,
Elmont, NY 11003

Printed in Italy. All prices are subject to
change without notice. (ISSN: 0003-8504)

Back To School: Architectural Education – the Information and the Argument

Guest-edited by Michael Chadwick

Δ

Architectural education is currently under pressure. Beset by destructive forces on both the outside and the inside, its resistance is being severely tested by the political ambushing of government and professional bodies as well as its own internal vermin and parasites. This seems to be the plaintive cry raised from institutions worldwide. For architecture, like many other forms of higher education in the last decade, has come under the scrutiny of bureaucratic assessment, overseen by regulatory and accreditation boards. This has led to the onset of a culture of 'professional management' and academic point-scoring; the internal point-scorers, gnawing away from the inside, being perhaps potentially more devastating than those disinterested bodies applying pressure from the outside.

So is architectural education in crisis? There is a very real danger that some institutions will stagnate – Peter Cook and Christine Hawley raise the frightening spectre of a weakening culture in architectural education across the UK as a whole. All institutions have their peaks and troughs, but are we in for a broader decline?

What, however, if the best architectural educators and their schools, at least, are able to create focus out of situations of potential conflict? What emerges out of this issue more than anything is leading educators' clear aptitude for action in the face of adversity. Whereas academics are so often perceived as preferring oral and written discussion over action, what surfaces here is, in fact, the reverse. Cook and Hawley at the Bartlett in London are engaged in a dynamic relationship between education and practice; Eleni Gigantes and Elia Zenghelis call for a renewed period of interest in architecture per se over text; and Leon van Schaik has been proactively addressing the shortfall in architectural education and education per se through his own involvement at RMIT at the highest level.

Education is a subject on which everyone has a view – every architect having been, or continuing to be, engaged with it at some level. More than any other topic, though, it asks us to question core assumptions: What does being an architect constitute? Is architecture a profession or a creative and research-based practice? What analytical and technical skills should be nurtured and provided through higher education? What should architecture's relationship be with practice, the conceptual and the written? Most intriguing, perhaps, is the very different take that all the contributors have on this single topic. Most heartening, though, for architectural education, is the fact that all the educators have come back to us with such impassioned responses. Ɑ

'Same old questions, same old answers, there's nothing like them.' — Samuel Beckett

This issue came about, initially, purely for my own selfish reasons. Following my experiences during my involvement within schools of architecture, I became very interested in the 'actual' yet not much talked about subject of architectural education. It became apparent to me that previous published statements on the subject seemed to emanate from people within institutions, statutory bodies or practice and, of course, were inevitably based on their own terms, 'waffling' on in an attempt to pass their own problems back on to the schools or to help exaggerate their own self-importance.

This led me to begin searching the shelves of numerous bookshops for a particular type of architecture book – one on education. Not an ordinary book, but a book of diversifying opinions, a book of varying intellectual thought, a book not simply of scientific pontificating words, a book not simply of masturbatory imagery, but a book on the education of a 'person' in the field of architecture. Amazingly, such a book cannot be found. And the intent of this publication is to remedy this.

In addition, throughout my career, juggling practice and teaching, I came into contact with so many young student architects who revealed to me the extent of their disillusionment, not just with the profession but also regarding their education, past and present. Mostly they would ask Why? Where? When? Who? and What is it all about, and how to continue doing it? Apart from the odd prospectus, occasional brief article within a weekly architectural magazine or websites on colleges, which all seem to be written for the accreditation bodies rather than for participating students, there is little out there to help the prospective student other than word of mouth. This publication attempts to address this, too.

In so doing, the issue provides five interviews with, and transcribed texts of conversations between, some of the most influential educators/heads of schools: Peter Cook and Christine Hawley; Anthony Vidler and Mark Wigley; Eleni Gigantes and Elia Zenghelis; Leon van Schaik and Tom Heneghan; and Paul Virilio, followed by shorter biographical articles by Beatriz Colomina, Peter Lynch, Neil Spiller, Dalibor Vesely, Brett Steele, Kevin Rhowbotham, Jonathan Hill and myself. In addition there are articles from key educators from countries of change: Yung Ho Chang (China), Iain Low, Lindsay Bremner and David Dewar (South Africa), and Vladislav and Liudmila Kirpichev (Russia). At the back is a listing of architectural institutions to help guide students in this international society of school education.

So this publication is about the educational process of architecture. It is not a self-promoting 'end-of-year review' but a source of ideas that discusses the reality of the dreams of the 'here and now' and the 'then and tomorrow'. It is not an egotistical book that attempts to encompass the be-all and end-all. Neither is it a concise issue with a full stop at 'the end'. It should be seen as a preface to starting a discussion, bringing the educational debate back on to the agenda. It does this by involving those on the front line – those who actually participate, live and breath it, who are passionate about architectural education, and who appreciate diversity of opinion and the range of discussions to be had.

It is therefore an attempt to start the stone rolling once again, and to shake off the complacent moss that has accumulated. Hopefully, after reading it, educators and those entering or participating in architectural education will stop and think for a moment about what there is to offer and the valid role of this subject – that there is option, variation and choice. ⚙

Peter Cook & Christine Hawley

It is generally accepted that if Alvin Boyarsky is God, then **Peter Cook** and **Christine Hawley** are the Adam and Eve of architectural education. Here, these two icons talk about the past, present and future of architectural education, and the problems still to be addressed in their Garden of Eden at the Bartlett School of Architecture.

Peter Cook: I sometimes find myself saying at lectures that most professors and, in particular, most professors of schools of architecture are doctrinaire, mainly telling students what not to read, what not to look at, whom not to listen to, where not to go and what not to do. This can be both a positive and a negative sign. However, I try to be very open about architecture because I am passionate about it. I believe that it has its own innate cultural strength and that the proscriptive position is very weak. Sure, one has one's own tastes and outputs, but if, like Christine and me, you're both designing and building architecture, as well as teaching it, then the sort of thing you like is made obvious by the nature of what you do. But then, simply to say you can only do such and such a thing leads to sterility in the end, and I am too fond of architecture not to keep in play the form and the ideas and their variations.

On this note, there is another thing I'd like briefly to introduce into the conversation – that I think architectural education is in great danger, and has been for the last 20 years or so, of being hijacked by those whose real interests are words rather than buildings.

I feel very strongly that architecture has a tremendous inherent culture of its own. Not just the tectonic aspect but the culture of responding to society, and responding to the state of the world and, really, all sorts of things. It is a mirror of society, and it responds with incredible richness. It is this aspect, in architectural education,

that is in danger of being hijacked by those 'academics' who are able, perhaps by virtue of their intellectual credentials, to make 'normal' architects feel very inferior.

Architects are always nervous that the world doesn't love them, and that nobody will commission them. The academics have exploited this vulnerability, implying that as a hands-on designer, the architect is inferior, because all he or she is interested in is substance. These academics maintain that their values and conversations, in that they refer to philosophy and cultural issues – and primarily to words – are much more important.

This academic influence on architectural education has come to dominate the present state of affairs for those who wish to participate in teaching architecture. In the US, and certainly even more so now in the UK, there is increasing pressure to publish, and not in any ordinary off-the-shelf publication, but within obscure accredited journals – academic, point-scoring journals. This has led to a situation where there appears to be a certain justification for appointing people to various high-level positions in architectural education based on the fact that they are qualified in a textual sense, rather than because they are interesting architects or are communicating specific architectural issues.

While this aspect of architectural education is far from new, it is currently increasing its grip, despite evidence of a backlash in the US where even some of the architectural historians and theoreticians are becoming disillusioned with it. Nevertheless, and disappointingly, here in the UK it is a trend that is still gaining momentum. And this is something of great concern for the future of architectural education.

Christine Hawley: Let me expand further on the role of the designer within architectural education here in the UK and in Europe. It is clear that the educational landscape has changed quite dramatically in the last ten to 15 years. In the UK 20 years ago, our schools were extremely well known for their focus on education within small private teaching structures, unlike the European campus arts schools which had huge numbers of students, with lecture classes of 350. For these European schools, real teaching went on in practice. Students were grounded in only a basic academic career, and only very small numbers actually graduated and entered into practice. Not until they went into practice did they really graduate.

So the teaching systems were extremely different but in both the European and UK systems of about 20 years ago, the designers were clearly dominant. The situation is now changing. I certainly agree with Peter in thinking that being in the discipline of the designer or even being in a practice is increasingly difficult within the present academically weighted architectural system, especially in the UK. The bureaucratic assessment process of the regulatory and accreditation boards is actually killing the designers off in UK schools. It is the historic problem of the way designers have been assessed over the past ten to 15 years that has caused tremendous friction about the way architects need to present their work in order to get the right ratings and therefore bring funding to the universities.

It should also be noted that these assessment criteria are based on the principles of scientific research, so there is a tendency for the institution suddenly to say that prospective teachers should publish their work in the conventional manner, in journals. If you look at who is getting appointed in the UK schools of architecture, it seems that what is required is evidence of the ability to get published in the accepted journals rather than evidence of actually being somebody who has any design credentials or profile in practice at all. This is the very big and very noticeable change in our schools and one that is particularly to blame for the current omission of practising architects from schools.

PC: I can see why certain well-known practising architects would say you can't be a practitioner and teach; their's is a very egocentric position and you know they would probably be bored by teaching. But I'm thinking of architects like Sverre Fehn and Tom Mayne, to take very current examples. Not only are they very good teachers but they are involved in building and architecture, and continue to be involved whenever they have students within their offices, or give seminars about how important are the process and the ideas involved in making the buildings. Unfortunately, while they are brilliant at this, there are a lot of people who are like them but don't teach. And there are all too many academics and the like, who will say, 'Oh well, we don't need people like them and they don't have any theories anyway', and will jump right into any available openings.

What really worries me is that these academics and theoreticians are moving into the design part of the schools. Now, you do get a few notable exceptions like Mark Wigley, who is a theory guy but who's a brilliant form critic – probably second to none – and just happens to be very interested in building, but there are not many like him around. I think Tony Vidler is in the same mould

Here in London: Tiger, Lion, Whale, Mouse, Leopard, Seal.

Above, left to right
Luke Chandresinghe, 'The Institute: Weights & Measure', 2004
The work has an unusual quality of power, carrying with it a spirit of connectivity that is surely key to architectural composition. In a year in which there were several people of high talent, Luke's work is some of the best remembered.

Samuel White, 'Homo Sapiens, Robo Sapiens, Homo Sapiens', 2004
This project makes an extraordinary transformation of Wells Cathedral, brings forth a new architecture that has something of the Gothic and something of the computer-generated world, and engages with particular theatricality.

Neil Tomlinson, 'Thorax Cybernation', 1994
Investigations into homeotypic insect mutants, nature's ultimate survival machine, inform a structural device whose physical dynamic produces an array of unpredictable structures.

Marjan Colletti, 'Comfortable Friends', 1999
Shaving his head, then Velcro-ing onto it a blanket containing his favourite soft-toy animals, the project was a hoot, but serious in the fact that it fed into Marjan's main 'Besking' project, embarking upon a fascinating architectural language that captured the special fluidity of soft materials and humour.

and, very importantly, they both run key international schools. They are managing to combine design and theory.

It's the detachment of the practice of architecture from society that is very dangerous for architecture schools where, instead of engaging directly with built form, students are expected to wade through a paper and a series of curricula readings rather than to design and, to be honest, the building is lucky if it ever comes into the conversation, never mind to fruition. I feel very strongly about this. Architectural education's cultural process is being hijacked and I would say this is a very worrying trend. Not that I don't write books myself; it's just that I don't claim that they matter more than the buildings, or architecture itself.

With regard to this aspect of detachment, some of the European countries prominent in architecture, countries we tend to regard as small such as Austria and Switzerland – which are seen as detached from the mainstream – are the sort of peripheral places that one watches. They approach very fast on the outside lane, producing some very good architecture and architects without having lots of magazines or books coming out; and I do wonder whether – and this probably sounds like a knee-jerk response – you detach the personality as soon as you detach the discussion on education from the business of architectural practice.

This seems to apply to the big architectural players like the US and UK whereas, if you take the smaller players, the really good architects in these countries and towns teach and their work stimulates theory that is articulated, producing a certain kind of school where the real personalities in architecture are building and teaching simultaneously. Even when teaching and practising, they never lose sight of their commitment to the business of architecture. But the big places tend to move away, and then you get some international institutionalised movement based on educational introversion and dictated by things like fashion.

CH: I wonder whether what you're alluding to, Peter, is almost like the old-fashioned tech course, where there was almost a sort of seamless conversation that went on within

practice, a conversation that also went on within the academic studio and in fact the boundaries were extremely blurred. Yet I wonder whether, particularly here and to some extent generally, architectural education has become extremely sanitised, become detached from the reality of making, become contrived and bureaucratically driven where the processes of making, thinking and intellectualising have in some way been rendered a synthetic exercise. That, for me, is one of the main criticisms of present architectural education.

PC: This introverted, intellectualised form of architecture has become its own profession and sometimes it almost doesn't seem to be interested in the actual profession of architecture at all.

CH: But it's dangerous because you get various, yet constant, criticisms from the profession about schools not producing a rational, comfortable student equipped to produce something that can move very quickly from the drawing board into a commercial context, and these may well be valid. So, recently, the thrust of the profession has culminated in trying to be overly descriptive and very prescriptive about the criteria you need to address in education, in a sense polarising the situation even more because what are described by the professional bodies are actually technical skills. Yet on the other hand it's being said by the bureaucratic university institutes that what is actually required is 'developed well-rounded thinking individuals', who will be even more theoretical. So what you're getting to is a very dangerous situation where the profession, on the one hand, demands that we produce at schools graduates who somehow seamlessly transfer into commercial practice and, on the other hand, the universities require schools to produce people who are almost overly academic. And then there are a few people caught in the middle, trying to do a balancing act, saying that actually what the school needs is a design basis and a design education in all its forms.

PC: And both sides are being caught up in this argument and the effect of the professional kickback is to dumb down. But the effect upon the schools is to treat the profession as dumb anyway, and with it the real essence of our argument which is actually about the architect and how the architectural idea develops. What they are responding to in cultural and technical terms, in cause-and-effect terms, is left almost like a dead art.

CH: It is also interesting to observe and contrast the UK with places like Milan, for example, where there's a culture of internism; where it is expected that after a number of years assisting or working in an architect's practice students go and set up their own practice with a project which has been given to them by the senior partners. This very rarely happens here in the UK. In these places a minor culture exists within the profession, of practitioners who have the quality of a 'tutor' and allow young people to experience the business of design work in a much simpler format. However, generally in the UK there seems to be a culture of extreme conservatism, of extreme caution. Here I have heard the most risk-averse opinions voiced anywhere – that you have to ensure that you take every precaution, ie UK practitioners equate risk with young people with very little experience.

PC: But this aversion to taking risks, to giving young people the opportunity to experiment in a practical way, is also creeping into schools, because courses are now getting taken over and there are onerous obligations to offer funky programmes run by oddball teachers who may not be qualified or run a practice. There's a lack of acknowledgment that there's a whole field of people like this who teach.

Actually I don't think that architectural education will die at all. I think it will flourish, but unfortunately it will have to flourish somewhere other than the UK.

You could say that ten to 15 years ago London really was a hotbed of enthusiasm and ideas. I mention the AA, out of which Christine and I came, but it also spawned students who believed they could become whatever they wanted to be. That was about 15 years ago and in certain other UK schools you probably also found about 25 studios with interesting people. Now you look at these same schools and what they do and promote is really boring. They are mostly being run by people who are incapable of running

anything. Maybe there needs to be monitoring of people in charge of architecture schools because, with a few notable exceptions, the current heads are not very interesting as educators, practitioners or theorists; they are in fact managers. And, what is worse, some of them are not only not architects, but they are not even interested in architecture!

Also what's interesting within the UK is that when you look at the ten most interesting architects in London, you have to ask why not one of them is teaching within a school of architecture there. There are a couple who are actually professors in Vienna, and you might discover that a third is a professor in the US or somewhere else, but not one holds a position within a school of architecture in London or the UK, which is where they ought to be – at home. Maybe this is because even if they are approached, they say, 'Look, I can't come in on every Thursday just like that; it's not compatible with my practice'; or they look at the derisory sum on offer and say, 'You must be joking!' But when they do tie in their practices with teaching commitments in schools in other parts of the world, they get treated well and paid well, and the students want to listen to them. They are given that mandate because they are good architects.

In a roundabout way, even London's contemporary architectural attitudes are being carried elsewhere. So I think the tendency to appoint theoreticians will increase and it is most likely that people who follow Christine and me – friends, fellow tutors and students – can't and won't get invited to be professors or move up the ranks unless they are considered useful in running undergraduate courses, filling in forms or complying with QA standards. I've painted such a depressing picture in the hope that with articles and publications like this, people, institutes and countries might say, 'Hey, wait a minute; we're losing control'.

CH: What you're describing really is the rise and rise of the QA function. QA culture comes from an overbearing bureaucracy, and when you look at what is imposed by the institution as opposed to the profession – and I use this word very cautiously because I think when one talks about the profession it is different from when one talks about extremely sophisticated individual architects – Peter is right that practitioners need to be involved far more in architectural education. I think that UK professional bodies do not actually fully represent the profession; they don't seem to realise that in trying to bureaucratise education they are not professionalising the schools; in fact, their actions are setting a range of criteria which actually take teacher and student away from what the schools ought to be trying to accomplish for the profession. Somehow there seems to be a belief that this actually incredibly abstract goal-chasing, which has very little to do with architecture, is somehow going to produce a better profession. I would argue that in ten years' time you will need a higher tier of architectural education because the graduates who will be coming through in the next generation are certainly not going

Below
Stephen Harty, 'Monument and Counterpoint', 1992
The work of Steve Harty, who in the early 1990s established a fantastically clear and challenging aesthetic of symbols, quoted machines and conceptual reference, in contrast to most English architecture, which emphasises details over concepts. His aim was to achieve the maximum effect, whatever the minimum means, recognising that architectural drawing is not just a representation of an external reality but also another reality with a specific influence on design.

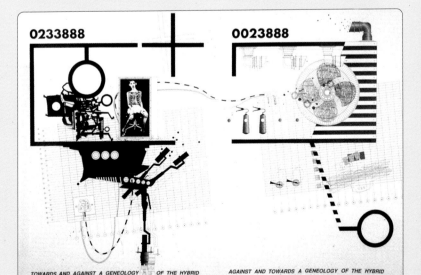

0233888   0023888

TOWARDS AND AGAINST A GENEOLOGY OF THE HYBRID   AGAINST AND TOWARDS A GENEOLOGY OF THE HYBRID

to be the perfection these institutes think they will be, and it will literally be a case of back to the drawing board if we are not careful.

PC: The other thing that one has to appreciate is that at the moment more people are still coming to London from other parts of the world, to study with us at all levels, because London is an interesting place architecturally. But as more and more courses open up in other parts of the world where English is the central language, people may well consider that it is more interesting to teach globally and there might be the reverse reaction. For example, Zaha Hadid is not actually teaching in London, she's teaching in Vienna. Now, if some bright spark says, 'I want to go and study with Zaha Hadid and unfortunately she doesn't appear to be teaching in London', they might just go and study in Vienna, especially as the EU makes movement possible, and tuition is free as well. This is just an extreme example, but if the English schools continue getting drearier and drearier, the well-informed and even the Mr and Mrs Averagely Informed, as well as the well connected, will say, 'Oh well, we can get what we want there instead!'

CH: Which would mean that we would all need to reconsider our present and future educational aspirations. You talked about the sort of people we attract at the Bartlett. We are very lucky because it does attract the extremely talented people, which is a great luxury and so teaching over here in the UK and at the Bartlett, especially for me, is a great privilege. But given the fact that these young people are so able and so resourceful and independent, they would be the ones to take advantage of the range of global opportunities. As UK architectural education becomes increasingly more rigid and obviously more costly, I can quite easily see those same students who come to us now actually looking at a much broader and wider field, and deciding that there really aren't that many varied and attractive schools here, and going elsewhere. Peter is right that if you fail to attract or stimulate these bright students with

Right
Matthew Springett, 'Manhattan Pig Farm', 1998
Hanging animals subdivide and screen the market hall and animate it when being moved or dissected. This spatial transformation is demonstrated through modular components that alter its shape and location in space. The pig farm continues to investigate the broader ethical and political issues related to the architecture of meat production and consumption.

what is on offer, we will have to face up to the fact that we're no longer going to attract the right students, and that this failure will inevitably affect the quality of our institutions and our profession.

PC: So, quite clearly, you think there should be a fusion of teaching and practice? Because if our professional-oriented establishments or universities had the courage to acknowledge what is going on, they would see it as a prime reason for good architects to be brought back into schools. Those architects who do now actually practise and teach wouldn't feel the need to get on an aeroplane and fly around the corner, especially when the same talented students are literally in the next street. At the Bartlett, we are getting very talented visiting tutors/lecturers, but actually in raw terms these people are international operators. You know my complaining like this is a cri de coeur. But only when the institutions and profession understand the value of the talented individuals we already have, on our doorstep and within the profession, will things begin to change.

CH: There may be some change already afoot, because there's much more lively discussion now, certainly within the RIBA and in a number of very influential institutes as well, about the nature of architectural education and that certainly wasn't the case five or ten years ago. The profession is slowly beginning to realise that there are huge problems facing the schools. To travel optimistically, we are beginning to see a culture in the schools that is slowly shifting from one of blame to one where the profession realises that it needs to act, possibly even redefine itself. If you look at the level of donations and funding required to maintain the enormous expenditure of universities, even of places like the Bartlett, there are now serious discussions about the capability and the viability of people building buildings, and these arguments are being published in mainstream, high-quality magazines. If the culture is shifting and the institution of architectural education is changing, then the climate will be ripe, maybe in the next four to five years, to encourage more practitioners to return to teaching and be heads of schools.

So there are some encouraging signs. But what Peter is saying is right; that one actually does have to speak out very, very forcefully against the context in which we find ourselves. Quite a number of mistakes have been made in the last couple of years and we are just beginning to start to rectify the situation. I'd like to be moderately optimistic that there will be a change in how professional architects who go into education to teach are perceived. However, the profession does have some things to answer for in the exploitation of students within architects' offices. I genuinely think there are some practices that do exploit, but I'd like to think they're in the minority. Yet we have practices that are immensely commercial, viewing students as a commodity, usually already equipped and ready to hit the deck running and turn out work rather than make considered judgements. Such practices simply use

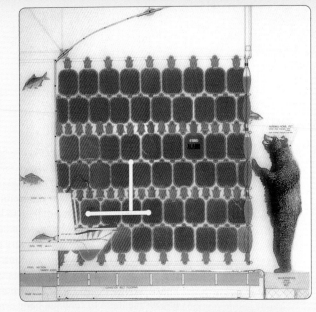

these students to do things that they have already mastered in their school work, rather than expanding their knowledge base. They will have to acknowledge that there are certain aspects of architectural education that have to be experimental! They cannot be synthetic – students can't be taught what a professional practice entails within a university context.

The solution to this devolves on managerial responsibility within the profession and its practices. The students need to understand the expectations of architects; they need to understand the relationship of the architect to the client and the other members of the team; and they need to understand the legal and contractual implications of what they are doing, and where they are situated within a multidisciplinary framework. In principle, this can be alluded to within the university, but it is only when you actually experience it in action that you really begin to understand it. When you are immersed in an actual 'building' job you see how substantially those assets of understanding how things work can affect the way you think and the positions you adopt.

Students need to take time out, away from the front line of production in practice, to observe how their colleagues and senior members deal with situations. After all, this is what happens in other professions such as medicine. You would never expect that, after a five-year medical course, somebody would walk straight out of university and put up a brass plate and take all the responsibilities of practice. Instead, they are rigorously supervised in post for several years and get first-hand advice, and experience of how their colleagues deal with situations. This is something that the architectural profession, I think, has neither the willingness nor interest to do! It claims it doesn't have the cash to do it, but

it doesn't have a sense of professional conscience to do it either, which is a shame.

There is another interesting aspect that follows from my initial comment, which is that all offices are now almost exclusively involved in production and would expect that when a student arrived, he or she would be pretty highly skilled at using a computer and adept at mastering the various software packages; if they can't, they're virtually unemployable. So the comment about the offices using young students as they do undergraduates and postgraduates to continually reproduce computer images actually lends the situation more urgency.

Unfortunately, this state of affairs actually started within architectural schools and it is this very emphasis on the use of computers and teaching their application which, while it is absolutely essential, has eradicated one of the things that in some places is becoming almost a dying art. That is, the skill of hand drawing. I find that when you talk to students who have primarily been drawing their ideas on a computer, you realise that they have lost an intellectual sense of totality. Unfortunately, what they are doing is just thinking about plans and sections, about fragments. As a result, what they find very difficult is to put those fragments together and arrive at a conventional understanding of what it is that they propose three-dimensionally and physically, which is, after all, what architecture is all about. I actually find this very disconcerting in the profession

Above right
Elizabeth Dow, 'Old Peoples' Home', Birkenhead,1993
Another influential project within the Bartlett and Unit 12, Elizabeth's 'Old People's Home' works with the everyday lives of its occupants. Instead of treating the occupants' actions as the strange or unexpected whims of the elderly, she accepts them, and their actions, as complexly normal but stereotypical.

Right
Abigail Ashton, Andrew Porter and Tony Smart, 'Mechanical Landscape(s)', 1994
Set in a redundant quarry south of Bad Deutsch-Altenburg, Austria, three projects establish topographical reference points with the town, the Danube and the major highways: 1) 'Bath/ Climbing School' develops from existing spa facilities and the surrounding rock face. Its constant state of change responds to the rise and fall in temperature of its steam rooms and the frequency and density of the climbers; 2) 'Pfaffenberg Hang-Gliding Centre' is a multilayered landscape of glass louvres, structure, service robot tracks, circulation routes and terraces that wrap around the quarry. This minimises turbulence to produce the lamina airflow needed for hang-gliding. In sunny conditions the aerofoils swivel to address the south, the louvres darken, and solar heat provides thermal up-currents; 3. The 'Ice Rink and Watersports Centre' takes on an ecological agenda, moving towards localised as opposed to zoned energy systems.

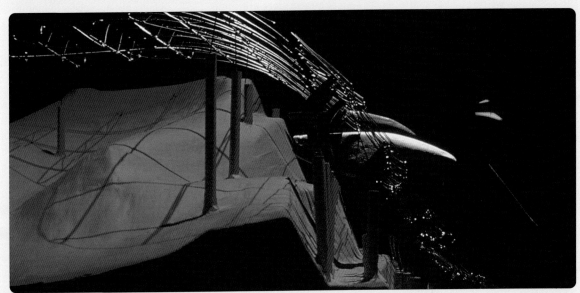

In both offices and schools, the use of relatively new, and continually renewed, digital technology has transformed the design process in varying degrees, putting into question the traditional techniques of hand drawing and modelling. In offices this has led to a heightened demand for digital skills, and in the schools the use of software programs, and their attendant aesthetics, has provoked a serious debate over the often too facile reliance on these aesthetics to generate designs. In summary, the question of architecture, once posed at the level of culture and form on the basis of fairly stable techniques and practices, is now opened up with no clear way being presented as to a choice between the 'good' past and the uncertain present.

This condition has been exacerbated as a result of the stylistic eclecticism forced by the Postmodern movement and the equally eclectic stylistic panoply now being resurrected by the new historians of the Modern movement. Schools of architecture, once more or less united around one or another philosophy or style, are now faced with a bewildering heterogeneity, even among their favourite heroes. How to choose among the neo-Expressionism of a Gehry or a Libeskind, the neo-high-tech of a Foster or a Rogers, the neo-Brutalism of a Botta or a Moneo, or the neo-Classical historicism of a Rossi or a Krier? Is the solution the programmatic late Modernism of a Koolhaas, the Duchampian irony of a Diller+Scofidio,

the-art in architecture so that they can decisively assert themselves around the world by producing remarkable buildings. We have to give them the capacity to change the discipline itself, to completely redefine the state-of-the-art. More than simply training architects how to design, we redesign the very figure of the architect. Columbia plays an international leadership role by being an open-ended laboratory for testing experimental ideas about the possible roles of the architect in society. The goal is not a certain kind of architecture but a certain kind of evolution in architectural intelligence.

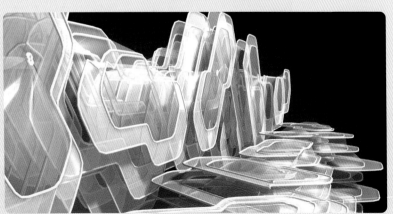

Role of the Architect

The architect is, first and foremost, a public intellectual, crafting the material world to communicate ideas. Architecture is a way of thinking. By thinking differently, the architect allows others to see the world differently, and perhaps to live differently. The perhaps is crucial. For all the relentless determination of our loudest architects and their most spectacular projects, architecture dictates nothing in the end. The real gift of the best architects is to produce a kind of hesitation in the routines of contemporary life, an opening in which new potentials are offered, new patterns, rhythms, moods, pleasures, connections, perceptions ... offered as a gift that may or may not be taken up.

Despite the generic image of the architect as the figure that heroically reshapes the built environment, the architect is involved in very little of what is built, and has very little control over even that little. It is probably the least heroic of the disciplines. Rather than to directly change the built environment, the art of the architect is to thoughtfully reflect upon the built environment with images, models and words, and even to understand constructed buildings as images, models and words – statements in an ongoing social discourse. The architect's buildings are a particular kind of polemical statement, placed in the city as might the books of a thoughtful novelist be almost accidentally placed in the Postconstructivism of a Hadid, the diagram architecture of an Eisenman? Or would it be the exploration of digital boundaries, from the topologies of a Ben van Berkel and Bos, the new geographies of MVRDV, the blobs of Lynn? Or again, the programmatic and pragmatic enquiries of a new generation of 'research' architects, suspicious of theory, rejecting of history and confident in the apparent authority of data, its flows and its animated forms?

But the real question, I believe, lies at a deeper level than these architectural differences, each of which, indeed, does offer very plausible answers to the formal and technical conditions of contemporary architecture. The problem lies rather in the political and, therefore, the social aims of the architectural culture as a whole, as they have radically shifted over the last 30 years from a postwar optimism in the social benefits of architecture, and the sense of service to a larger community than that of the client and developer, to much-reduced claims and a concentration on the aesthetic and technological constraints of the single building. For while Modern architecture's beliefs in the present, in progress and in 'modernity' as a project were firmly based on the ideal of social betterment through architectural and urban change, present goals are limited by the disenchantment that followed so many apparently failed experiments in social engineering. The optimism of postwar reconstruction, dashed against charges of authoritarianism from the Left and economic stringency from the Right, quickly fell prey to the hedonism of style-mongering and the withdrawal of the architectural profession from large-scale social projects.

We are now left with a distrust of architecture itself that extends both to its internal formal and aesthetic procedures, as well as to its social role as a whole.

In retrospect, it seems that, certainly in the US, the ideals of Modern architecture were too closely identified with dominant aesthetic modes – the International Style – and therefore far too susceptible to the challenge of aesthetic, as opposed to social, confrontation. What began as a more sophisticated discussion of collage, of complexity and contradiction in the 1970s, became a ready instrument for the demolishing of the aspirations of Modern architecture itself. The easy assumption of the 'failure' of architecture in the service of society, fed by the demolishing of prominent social architecture projects (for example the housing development of Pruitt Igoe designed by Minoru Yamasaki, whose reduction to rubble marked, according to Charles Jencks, the end of the Modern Movement and the beginning of the Postmodern Movement) allowed for the substitution of style over substance.

a newsstand in a railway station, embedding the thought of something different amongst all the routines, opening up the momentary possibility of a detour. The architect crafts a hesitation that acts as an invitation to think differently.

Academicism

Concerns about academicism are normal but contradictory. Part of the magic of architecture is the way it mixes theory and practice, academic and professional, detachment and engagement. The fact that so many contemporary teachers base their work on publications and exhibitions without building much is not a big deal and it's not news. It has been the very basis of architecture as a discipline ever since we argued in the 15th century that the architect is an intellectual, the one who makes drawings of buildings rather than the buildings themselves. And just as most architects would like their drawings to be turned into buildings, paper architects have a habit of turning into builders.

It's not so much that they change – become more serious, more practical, or more responsible as they get older. Rather, the understanding of building evolves. Things that seemed impossible become possible, and unbuilt projects contribute significantly to that evolution. After all, architects don't just design buildings. They also design the climate within which buildings are seen, which usually means a full-time campaign of lectures, writings and exhibitions. As public intellectuals, architects use whatever medium they can to change the way we see our world. And building itself is understood as a form of publication, presenting a certain set of ideas to the world, creating a climate for the perception of other buildings. Look at Peter Cook, one of the great teachers, both in the academy and in the way his early decades of paper projects, polemical exhibitions and publications created the possibility for himself and others to finally build. And where would we be without the irreplaceable wisdom of Cedric Price?

Modern architecture's style – its minimalism, housing typologies, refusal of tradition and history – all became fair game in the return to what were supposed to be the tried and tested aesthetic values of a good-old past. The signs and symbols of history were adduced to refer to humanism and, therefore, populism; the virtues of the classical style and the pitched roof were raised once more to mask a wholesale rejection of social reform programmes. The problem now became one first raised in the equally eclectic 1830s by the Romantic historian Hubsch: 'In what style should we build?', as opposed to, for example: 'In what ways might architecture work to better society?'

In this context, the crisis in education has to be described as part of a larger crisis of confidence

in the public realm – a crisis willingly sustained by large-scale business interests and the drastic withdrawal of national, state and local government from any basic support for social housing, public facilities and, more recently, public schools, health-care institutions and so on – all programmes that were once seen as fundamental to the repertory of Modern architecture. And where such institutions do receive funding, there is rarely an interest in the architectural qualities of the resulting construction, let alone investigation into the alternative possibilities of spatial organisation or research into the technologies of conservation.

At the same time, the ability of architecture to operate on the spectacular, as opposed to the programmatic, level is being demonstrated by high-profile competitions for ideas and signature buildings that are claimed to raise the profile of institutions and cities, and even to foster economic development with the implication that architecture is now understood as an aesthetic rather than social good.

In many disciplines, such a situation would present a crisis – of nerve, of sponsorship, of judgement. In architecture, however, and looking historically, we might say that such a situation has been permanent for more than three centuries. That is, in the history of architectural education, such a situation has occurred some 10 times since the middle of the 17th century, for

Those that aim at what cannot yet be built often create the shift in thinking that allows building practice to evolve. But the reverse is also common. Dedicated builders often become very reflective and speculative later in their careers, reaching beyond what can be done to what might be done.

Further, the mix between speculative and practical keeps shifting. At Columbia, for example, much of the experimentation over the last decade involved heading deeper and deeper into electronic space, seemingly leaving behind the world of actual building. But many of the teams went so far into electronic space that they came out the other side having developed such an expertise in digital modelling that they were able to pioneer new techniques of construction, detailing and prototyping, which has led to a wave of innovative research into new materials and fabrication. There has been a refreshing re-engagement with the wider art of building, aligned with a new kind of engagement with questions of social programme, economics and politics. This is the whole point of the academy, allowing the discipline to detour away from its default settings in order to find new settings, new forms of professional, technical and even ethical practice.

Academicism is therefore a crucial part of the survival mechanism of the discipline. It is a space for exploration and redefinition. All sorts of experiments must take place, most of which will never lead to a direct change in the professional practice of architects. But the wide range of potential directions created in the academy, combined with the wide range of ongoing research within professional offices, creates the space within which the discipline can think through its future. Graduates are an

different reasons and in different contexts of society and practice. But in general, education has posed a 'question' at moments when there has been a radical shift in the nature of society envisaged as the 'client' of architecture, a change in the technology of building practices or, more internally, an emerging change in the nature of theory or, more internally still, in the techniques of representation and signification.

Though all of these causes are linked, not all have become issues at the same times throughout modern history. Thus we might trace the origin of the question of architectural education to the attempts of newly self-conscious and politically centralised states, led by France and Britain in the 17th century, to gain control of the theories and techniques of production.

In France this led to the foundation of the Académies royales under Louis XIV and his minister Colbert, and the appointment of a coveted list of architectes royales to administer the principles and practices of the art. In Britain this task was left to the more loosely state-sponsored Royal Society. In both cases the philosophy of the day (Descartes in France, Locke in Britain) led to the appointment of geometers and mathematicians as 'chief' architects –

François Blondel in France, Christopher Wren in Britain. In both cases the disintegration of a mythical belief in the perfection of antiquity resulted in the invention of codes of proportion, historical evidence and architectural practice based more on contemporary needs than on ancient mythology.

The Enlightenment reinforced this movement, and thus was created the first independent private architecture school in Europe, the Ecole des Arts founded by the architect Jacques-François Blondel (no relation to his predecessor), who was also the main contributor to Diderot's great Encyclopédie in matters of architecture. Blondel was responsible for the establishment of the first systematic architectural curriculum, one that has persisted throughout multiple changes of content but which, in form, still holds sway today. This is the system that divides the subject of architecture into many small parts, each considered as an entity in itself, each forming a small 'discipline' within architecture around its own concerns. Thus Blondel offered courses in professional practice, history, theory, building techniques, site organisation and, later, structures.

He also added courses for the future clients of architecture – builders and contractors – to enable them to understand the intricacies of the discipline they were involved in. But the centre of architectural education in

asset to the profession precisely because they can detour away from the traditional assumptions of the profession. The relatively recent emergence of university training for an architect, in addition to the usual system of training through apprenticeship, was the emergence of a new creative space within which the discipline could redefine itself, a space of experimentation, mutation, speculation, testing, criticism and analysis. This space, like the discipline itself, is fragile and needs continuous but delicate care – like a garden or a good meal. It is too easily squandered when schools mistakenly assume that their role is to simply reinforce the profession's current image of itself, and thereby unwittingly threaten the profession by blocking its capacity to evolve.

History and Theory
In recent decades, the US has clearly played the major role in the cultivation of experimental history/theory, while Europe has played the major role in cultivating the construction of buildings by a new generation of designers, and this difference is reflected in the way the schools in each are organised. Yet all of the more than a hundred schools of architecture in the US

privilege design over history/theory. Everything is organised around the design studio, as it should be. If architecture schools are the laboratories in which the field of architecture negotiates its future, the design studio is the laboratory at the heart of the laboratory.

The precise relationship between history/theory and what happens in the studio varies from school to school and should perhaps be ever shifting within each school. For example, all the different parallel and overlapping programmes at Columbia – architectural design, urban design, historic preservation, urban planning and real estate development – have design studios, but the proportion of time spent on history/theory varies between programmes. Yet even this moving line between history/theory and studio has become blurred within the school, with seminars, lectures, workshops and symposia increasingly taking place within the studios. Design is simply a form of expert research. Again, the main point is to insist that the designer is a certain kind of thinker.

Architecture is a set of endlessly absorbing questions rather than a set of clearly defined objects with particular effects. This is its central attraction. Objects standing clearly and still in front of us for so long that they act as society's models for clarity and stability, are actually relentlessly elusive and mysterious. If architects have been arguing about architecture and developing their expertise for thousands of years, there is no common

Eleni Gigantes & Elia Zenghelis

Through a weave of edited and reappropriated texts, the influential educators and urban thinkers Eleni Gigantes and Elia Zenghelis curate their ideas on modern and metropolitan architectural education. The discussion is illustrated with the 'Simple Hearts' project, executed by Pier Vittorio Aureli and Javier Rojas Rodriguez, under the supervision of Zenghelis at the Berlage Institute in the Netherlands.

Pier Vittorio Aureli, Javier Rojas Rodriguez
'Simple Hearts'

'A cloud of blue incense smoke rose up to Félicité's room. She opened wide her nostrils as she breathed it in deeply, in an act at once sensual and mystical. She closed her eyes. Her lips smiled. Her heartbeats grew steadily slower, fainter every time, softer, like a fountain running dry, like an echo fading; and as she breathed her last, she thought she saw, as the heavens opened, a gigantic parrot hovering over her head.'
— Gustave Flaubert, Un coeur simple (1872)

Beyond the Generic City

We have no vested interests because we are sure that, in a very honest way, there are no problems. In recent years we have become newly enthralled with research in architecture and urbanism. This is an issue that has gained considerable attention, mainly as a response to the effects of economic globalisation, political turmoil and commercial allure. Research has been turned fundamentally into a problem-solving operation, where all of the work is conducted within a specific framework defined by the vested interests of a client/programme. We cannot afford to dismiss research, but in order to be a tool in the service of, rather than an obstacle to, new discoveries, research must be driven to push the limits of the problem by challenging its original question and looking at conditions outside its framework so as to discover things that were not there in the beginning. Vested interests, together with problem solving, seriously threaten the production of ideas that strike at the core of our civilisation's most important issue – an idea of the city.

In past years, an idea of the city has been replaced with an image of the city. The vital foundation for our professional practice is today entirely absent. As a response to this situation, we need to revise history, revisit failed attempts and replenish our practice with another idea of the city as its utterly indispensable ingredient. This will mean establishing a discipline – a set of limitations that could allow us to concentrate on a very specific framework, and deliberately to ignore all remaining issues that are irrelevant for the described goal. This is a liberating action because, in such a rigorous separation, the professional practice of urbanism (which is specific and bottom-up implemented), and architecture (which is generic and top-down implemented), can be cleared up.

Gigantes Zenghelis Architects (GZA) typify an architectural practice with its roots firmly grounded within the field of education. Here, Eleni Gigantes and Elia Zenghelis survey their views on both education and architecture through the reappropriation of earlier texts, articles and quotations, both published and unpublished. These serve to produce a history of their thinking, culminating in a summary of their present position in the context of an overview of the past.

The 1980s[1]
The Office of Metropolitan Architecture (OMA) unit at the Architectural Association (AA) in London functioned as a polemical laboratory that sought to re-examine and redefine orthodox dependencies on notions of reality and normality – to assess the possibilities for architecture in the metropolis. The aim of the 'diploma 9' unit was to rediscover and develop a form of urbanism appropriate to the final part of the 20th century; to generate new types of architectural scenario that exploited the unique cultural potential of high-density living, and to produce a critique and rehabilitation of the metropolitan lifestyle.

The unit carried a torch for Modernism. While having no interest in rehabilitating its purist forms, it preserved many of its ambitions and shared such determinist notions as that architecture can, and should, provoke lifestyle. But instead of architecture explicitly defining a single utopian lifestyle – as some functionalist ideals implied – the approach was pluralist, advocating the creation of stimulating settings in which disparate lifestyles could coexist. The task of the then 'today's' architecture was not to raze and rebuild the city, but through selective and strategic intervention to re-equip it with the new facilities that would allow mass society fully to exploit the potential of our times – not least for hedonism.

With a sufficient density of population, and with novel juxtapositions of different activities, catalytic reactions set in, which spontaneously generated new and ever more exciting activities and forms of social intercourse. The architect's role was to provoke and manipulate such effects, and the unit then worked with students on this principle. It was important to treat architecture and culture as intertwined, and since a concern for the masses and the nature of an uncondescending mass culture necessitated a historical perspective, seminars, often on recent history, were essential components of the unit's design investigations.

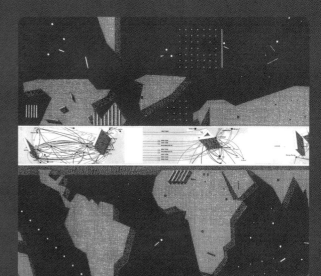

Entities
Today, as governments transform into softer and more invisible institutions, infrastructure exists in stark contrast, where far from being invisible it has been established, and rarely contested, as a new form of governance – where all entities within our built environment are left with two options (neither of which is desirable): to converge into infrastructure and be digested, or to depart and thus remain in a vast sea of anonymity. In this way, the work presented in the following plates understands the primordial necessity of entering different organisations and relationship principles among entities. It serves as an artifice that explores such plausible principles among an abstract territory composed merely of two kinds of entity – points and lines. Points (architecture) constitute the indirect consequence of lines (infrastructure), where their present relationship is the result of decisions taken, but also of those that were never taken.

Paraphrasing Kandinsky, architecture is the ultimate contrast to infrastructure. Architecture carries within itself only tension, and can have no direction, whereas infrastructure necessarily partakes both of tension and direction. In the relationship between these entities, and the new ones that can emerge from their confrontation, is something that must become the most important issue of our new century, in order to stop them becoming new forms of governance.

Our interest here is not to define what infrastructure is, but what it means. What does it mean for infrastructure to be the convergence/departure point of different technologies like the high-speed train and fibre-optic channelling, among others? What do infrastructures activate in territories whose geographies seem highly uncertain? We must speculate further on how this significance is being, or could be, made widely accessible. Taking points (architecture) and lines (infrastructure) as the bare essentials of our idea, its development can be that of a bifurcated path where their linear logic and blunt juxtaposition can start to give way to a completely new grammar.

This led the unit to formulate new ways of designing and drawing that attempted to shape and depict buildings that would be graphically explicit of their role in the city, and of the social instability they were intended to provoke. Typically, the projects were boldly massed as a collage of separate elements, while inside these envelopes interiors were loosely defined and space and activity agitated by sensuous curves and violent graphic slashes and interpenetrations. The resultant plans often seemed neither very usable nor spatially comfortable. The unit, like others at the AA, quickly became identified with a particular style. To avoid the risk of freezing within a set style, we stressed analysis of programme and the elaboration of imaginative scenarios to inform the design. But no matter how analytical and theoretical the approach, it can still run the risk of collapse into a merely consumable style.

The 1990s[2]
The GZA method of teaching is naturally an evolving continuum of the OMA unit, so if the work is recognisable this is evidence of continued and refined thinking rather than trial-and-error sequences. So, its similarity to the OMA unit's processes is natural, given that we were part of OMA and are now both GZA. We make no apology for this as we often feel that something graphic is intimated when architecture is likened to OMA and that the architecture of OMA remains. In our case, it needs to be recognised that OMA was only

relevant to GZA as a historical chapter, relating to a certain time, and has been an uneasy ghost to lay to rest ever since.

The student work is again continuing, and again refocusing on the city. Although at the time we were engaged in the earlier OMA unit projects the city was something people feared, today they embrace it. We continue to aim to restore respectability to an interrupted chapter in Modern architecture – to provoke a new mutation.

The aim of our project briefs now is to challenge students to change them – to remould them to their own briefs – work that has its basis in our manifesto, creating architects who want to go out and change the world. This is a logical development that stems from the students' impatience to become practising architects, and to start thinking now, while still in college, about the actual ideas and manifestos they themselves will take with them in order to change the world or recreate it.

For us, the students' work must move away from original projects that are plausible only in the 'extreme' world of the ideal – a fictional perfect world, overflowing with plenitude – to a belief that they are producing work that can be realised. The aim is to develop beyond this doctrinairism; as practising architects we insist on being undogmatic and operative, and in our affirmation of reality we search for qualities within it. Thus we do not get the students to define themselves, nor to work to agreed limits; we strive, instead, for the development of new and diverging directions. It is the personalities of the students involved, each of whom brings his or her own innate themes, talents and emphases, that serve to expand

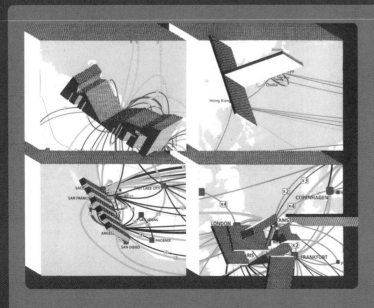

Another Idea of the City
The small universe of entities that we have previously defined gives way to four scenarios that have the potential, because of their critical differences, to embody another idea of the city.

I The Exasperated Equality scenario has looked with envy upon the development of highly evolved lines elsewhere. This is a region constantly at the edge of the civilised, with volatile and heterogeneous points standing in close proximity to each other within an unconcealed environment where equal distribution, but with different associations, takes place.

II The Atlantic Hedge scenario has long been an impenetrable barrier currently being altered in its morphology, where the aggressive confrontation between urban penetration and ecological preservation plays a key role.

III The Objet Trouvé scenario is undergoing major structural and spatial changes that induce an arrangement of its territory as a still-life picture, where all elements seem to share an animated topic/interest but are nevertheless stagnant and disengaged from each other.

IV The Cartesian Stretch scenario embodies the highest profile and busiest line in the region. It is essentially a stretching line that links vast and previously isolated points into a close-knit and fast-growing area where previous deficiencies are turned into great opportunities.

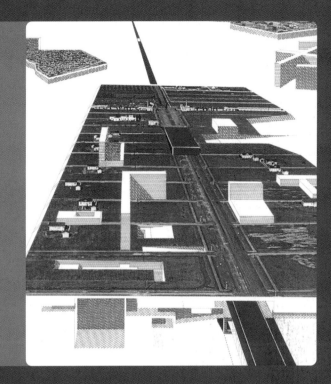

Latency and Throughput
Even within the four different scenarios described
earlier, the essential components of our idea –
points (architecture) and lines (infrastructure) – are
still made visible and available. We should further
say that these components show a great degree of
efficiency, since they produce critical differences
within each scenario, and accessibility, as they are
facilitating a relationship among them.

Both issues allow us to establish a parallel with
storage-area network (SAN) engineering that deals
with the massive data growth and the great
demands on infrastructure for storing it and making
it available. Latency is a concept used in SAN
engineering to define 'a potential that finds itself in
a dormant or hidden stage'. Throughput is defined
as 'the amount passing through a system from input
to output over a period of time'. Together, latency
and throughput constitute an extraordinary idea of
the city, where both elements are in synergetic
relationship, constantly serving and servicing each
other, and persistently seeking to overcome the
city's fragile equilibrium.

the projects. Each project is a new beginning,
to which we and others bring all our individual
themes and agendas.

The prime reason, we believe, that people
are unable to shake off the history of OMA is that
basic architectural student projects always
contain certain iconography and signs and,
combined with the graphics required to depict
the architecture we talk about, there is little one
can do about this. The misunderstanding of the
projects, primarily due to their unmistakable
language of graphic representation, has been
one of our biggest disappointments.

The work is unquestionably modern:
Modernism of a progressive nature combined
with irreversibility of strategy and conviction;
Modernism without dogma, where design is
created in tandem with an 'x'-factor – the
unforeseeable – giving the tension that only
develops over time. It seems ideas are strong in
proportion to their unbuilt grey areas of
freedom – the ability to engage with the
unforeseeable. They are supple in as far as they
resist controlling the uncontrollable, and they
are strategic.

Projects are only a freezing point in a
condition of fluidity, and the bold clarity and lack
of compromise required for a new idea to
materialise is also a moment of temptation. It is
easy to see how, at this point, a rigid imposition
of ultrapersonal, or alien, ideas can introduce
the aridity of dogma. It is a wrong step that is
only a hair's-breadth away.

Thus strategies emerge inside the material, as
a starting point but with no solutions. Neither the
students nor we ourselves can predict the end when
we begin. Ignorance and unexamined prejudices are
the first thing challenged by the new, and the difficulty
is to respond and not to react – to keep pushing back
one's own barriers and to be analytical. In other
words, you explore and sometimes invent, but you
usually start off somewhat in the dark and are often
surprised. Behind this is a conviction that a successful
project will take on a life of its own, beyond the
unwitting narrowness of our own projections and
inventions. It is a product of the work, but ideally,
after a certain point, it will escape from the blind
spots through its own momentum and energy, and
we will all then learn from it.

We will also learn by listening to the messages that
emanate from outside the world of architecture –
architecture can, and should, contribute to the world.
And this does not depend on how harmonious it looks;
there is no longer a consensus on this sort of thing.
It may even stress its functional leverage, or refer to
its cultural authority. However, all demand that it's
sensible and pertaining to their way of life – these are
our clients; they remind us that cities have no ideas
on how to respond to these conditions and express a
belief that we do.

Critical intervention of the imagination – functional
means being critical, able to retain a certain level
of provocativeness. It means working with ideas
that do not conform to either fashion or taste – or
to any other ephemeral system of oppression.

We work not in the field of Modernism in

The Servant
The construction of our ideas model depends heavily on the feeble relationship between two basic components: the line (infrastructure) is characterised as a servant in a blissful state of innocence – giving so much in return for so little. Such a servile attitude plays a crucial role since it establishes a regime of equalities where symmetry is a territorial consequence that determines many factors such as plot dimension and serviceable area. The servant is an underground line with enormous spatial demands, regardless of its concealed character. This represents a new monumentality, always on the verge of dissolution.

In the servant everything is dormant. Its heart is built of cables, ducts and pipes that demand great attention (beyond refusal or celebration). The rest of its substance is absolute emptiness, spatially defined as buffer zones that resist penetration. Typical extruded aluminium components, double glazing and neoprene gaskets land before floor and ceiling on an anti-vibration pneumatic flatbed that provides easy installation and dismantling.

The New Millennium[3]

It has not been accepted – ever since Kant – that there is an unbridgeable gulf between reality in itself and reality as it appears to us. That our possibilities of knowing have more to do with our own apparatus than with the 'nature' of reality.

Indeed, the persistent propaganda of the past decade – calling for an objective 'reality' to figure at the centre of the architectural discourse – has been mystifying; an indefensible affectation over time became a tyranny – and a self-eviction from our own humanity; a 'reality' seen as truth, underpinning every architectural enterprise, an 'ideal' mission, even a completed project, which needs no tampering with, only 'articulation'. Reality as paradigm, only to be 'mapped' and 'branded' (now on the political correctness decline). Despite pretensions of scientific 'method', it is a random sampling process of gratuitously selected contextual information (called 'research') and gathered in the name of 'realism'. Avoiding the painful confrontation with architecture, it is projected as 'the alternative', a ready-made that procures the project; its so-called objectivity 'protects' it from the anachronistic architectural vice of self-indulgence. Is this not a cover-up, the frustrating sight of architects fleeing from their own prerogatives? In the scientific world, mapping has defined objectives, based on inspired speculation. With architects it has become the penultimate manifestation of groping in the dark, an exercise resting on hope, with 'research' becoming a mantra conjuring inspiration.

As for the more recent criticism of this position – now on the rise from a supposedly leftist new engagement – it, too, has an uncanny spinelessness that is reminiscent of 1968, even as it evokes the spectre of revolution. Our tragedy is that we live under an acute sense of illusion without any sense of disillusion. There has been no revolution, only loss: we are victims in a void – inhabitants of the political barbarism of our posthumanist 'sophistication'.

If there is a discrepancy between such interpretations and my view of reality, I admit it: this patronage of 'reality' is a call for architecture to be either 'realistic' or 'utopian', and I believe that the real discrepancy is to be found between the ambition of these views and the instrumentality of architecture. As for inspiration, it is a transaction grounded on insight, cognisance, imagination: a lost art based on a humanist tradition that the technocratic servitude of our age is in the process of dismantling.

Through the ages, imagination has been the ability to visualise hearsay, to represent the unknown, to postulate on a future absence and to remake what is summoned in myth or an idea in the solitude of one's psychology. The gift to represent that which is in the mind's eye: what one has heard of but never seen. It is the ability to come to terms with the conflict that arises in our order of existence, when the latency of a 'future form' is perceived among our world of references and

Our interest in architecture is 'relative' in the sense that it is limited to architecture in itself: we don't believe that the tomes of exegetic literature about it that have flooded the market deserve the forests destroyed to provide the paper.

Notes
1 Text partially reappropriated from an interview text given by Elia Zenghelis, Rem Koolhaas and Zaha Hadid to Peter Buchanan within the Architectural Review issue titled The Architectural Association School of Architecture, October 1983.
2 Text partially reappropriated from an interview text given by Elia Zenghelis and Eleni Gigantes to Yannis Aesopos and Yorgos Simeoforidis within the journal El Croquis , No 63, 1994.
3 Text partially reappropriated from text written by Elia Zenghelis entitled 'Text and architecture: architecture and text', to be published within a forthcoming book.

requires a technique to materialise it: the discourse that will give form to the conjectures of our psychology.

Nevertheless, this lost art is as recoverable as Proust's time – through the discovery of the power of reinterpretation: the passage from the state of reminiscence to the state of materialisation. It can be practised and sharpened through learning to 're-present' and reconstitute reality – as practice. It is the most fertile and gratifying (albeit difficult and painstaking) occupation one can creatively engage in, ie the supremacy of the synthetic over the real and the ability to invent the forms with which the passage from one to the other can be realised.

At the same time this recoverability is essential to re-establish the immediacy of the object over the secondary discourse of hermeneutics: as the primary discourse of the discipline, architecture possesses a direct vocabulary and syntax that communicate what it is by itself and without the intermediary of explanation.

Our interest in architecture is 'relative' in the sense that it is limited to architecture in itself: we don't believe that the tomes of exegetic literature about it that have flooded the market deserve the forests destroyed to provide the paper. This stems from our immutable conviction that all the so-called

higher arts (of which architecture still is one) have an inherent 'idiolectic' property that gives them a unique 'absoluteness', with a self-sufficient vocabulary and syntax of their own. We mentioned literature because its objective materiality is the text and this makes the argument self-evident. But what applies to literature applies to all arts and, hence, to architecture. They all have their own inherent text. While at the service of societies and their politics, they possess a critical autonomy, being a law unto themselves and only unto themselves, with which they transcend their role and through which they become critical. This is their 'primary' discourse and that of architecture is matter: its vocabulary and syntax are the vocabulary and syntax of matter. Nothing can be said about the nature (and sense) of architecture that architecture itself cannot say more immediately – and better. Moreover, as it continuously 'rethinks' its own inheritance in order to 'mirror' the world it serves and represents, it becomes de facto critical; its critical instrumentality lies in being there – and being there is its only explanation.

To summarise, since good architecture is de facto critical, we firmly believe that, except for a compulsory, uncritical and detailed history, limited to facts, dates and (exhaustive) illustrations, there is nothing of importance to write about it. Architecture is matter and architects need only work with the vocabulary and syntax of matter. Their role is to design buildings, the acknowledged quality of which will be their sole value and, as always, the only reason for architects to be remembered. To paraphrase Stravinsky and since (like music or literature) architecture is absolute from the moment it assumes as its calling the expression of the meaning of discourse, it leaves the realm of architecture and has nothing more in common with it.

In the present void, this is more urgent than ever. We have gone full circle; so in conclusion we paraphrase one of Rem's old quotes: 'In a situation where architecture has become a concrete glass slipper nobody even wants to try on any more', the next generation must be 'devoted to reconquering architecture's powers of seduction through the refinement and implementation of its own principles'. To do this now, it will have to eject the redundant baggage of 'content' and, by focusing purely on its form, consider architecture as text. ⚙

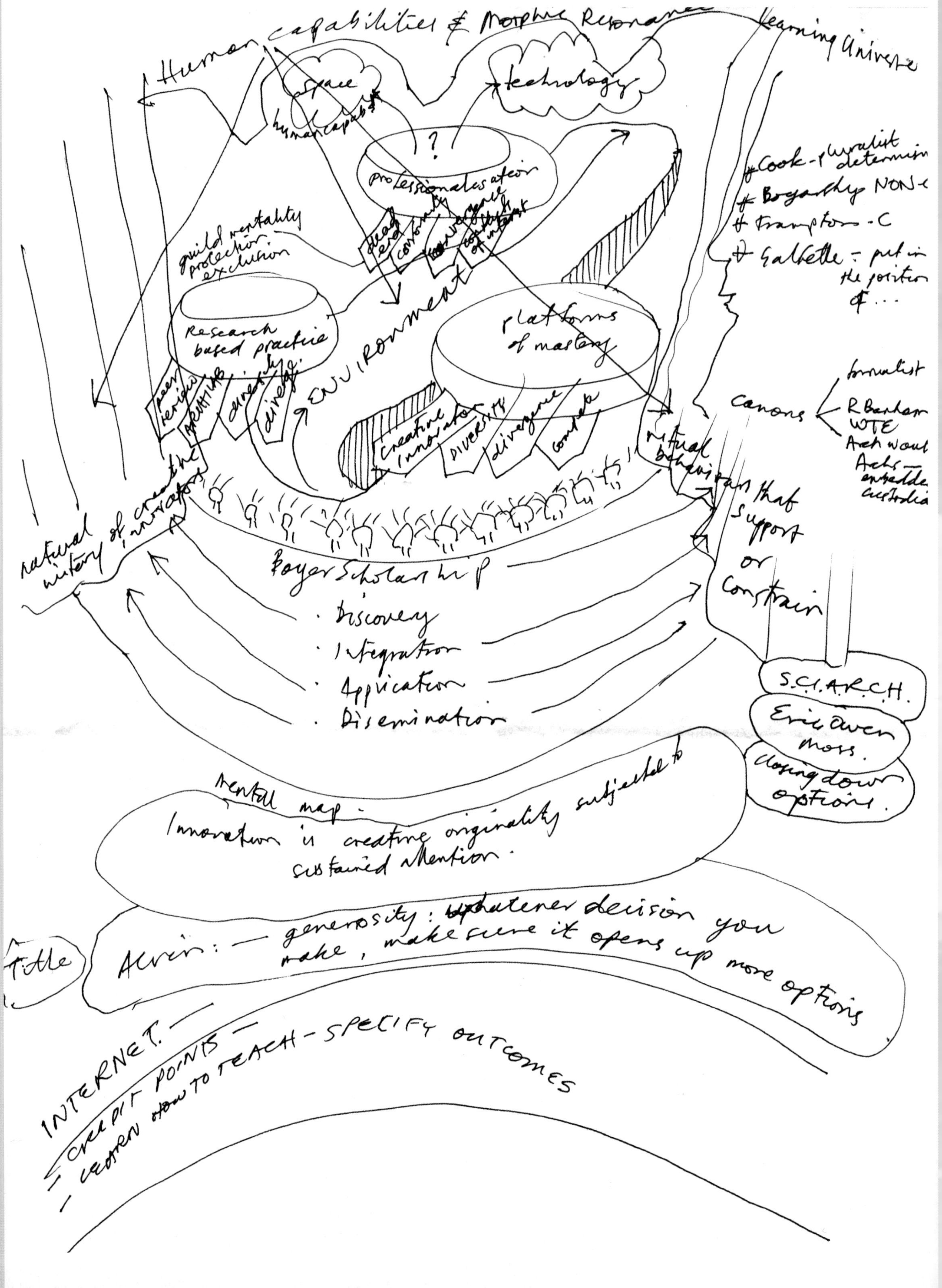

Human capabilities & Morphic Resonance   Learning Universe

space
human capabs
Technology

?
professionalisation
guild mentality
protection
exclusion

dead end?
community of interest

Cook- pluralist determin
Bogarthy NONE
Frampton - C
Galbette = put in the position of ...

ENVIRONMENT

Research based practice
peer review
mentoring
diverse
diverse

platforms of mastery
creative innovation
DIVERSITY
divergence
complex

ritual behaviour that support or constrain

Canons
formalist
R Banham
WTE
Arch Woul
Achs —
ecstatic
australia

natural of creative history of innovation

Boyer Scholarship

- Discovery
- Integration
- Application
- Dissemination

S.C.I.A.R.C.H.
Eric Owen moss.
Closing down options.

Mental map.
Innovation is creative originality subjected to sustained attention.

(Title)   Alvin: — generosity: whatever decision you make, make sure it opens up more options

INTERNET. —
CREDIT POINTS —
OPEN HOW TO TEACH - SPECIFY OUTCOMES

Leon van Schaik and myself share the heritage of an approach to architectural education that flourished at the Architectural Association (AA) School of Architecture in London for two decades, from the mid-1960s to the mid-1980s. There was something about that approach that was uniquely fitted to producing leading architects and educators – a disproportionately high number of architects and educators who have reputations for being involved in intellectual change in their fields emerged from the school during those years. In Australia, this has been particularly true, with the deans and professors of almost all architecture schools being AA graduates of that period.

Yet, institutionalised higher education at universities is very different from the deconstructed, unscripted, agile and broad-

predescribable situation. In the current university milieu, everything that was then done to such great effect is almost impossible. I have taught architecture in five countries over a period of nearly 30 years, and find the situation of education in Australia – a 'young country' – to be surprising in its embrace of convoluted managerial structures. The AA was innocent of this. There was no management structure. People made and discussed architecture, not committee resolutions. Through the contemporary labyrinth, though, Leon van Schaik has been able to navigate a clear and individual route. At the Royal Melbourne Institute of Technology (RMIT) he has established a programme that does not replicate the AA system, but which interweaves the principles of the AA programme into the particular educational and professional context of the institution. At the University of Sydney I'm beginning to do the same. However, since the educational and professional

Leon van Schaik & Tom Heneghan

Leon van Schaik and Tom Heneghan are two of the foremost figures in architectural education in Australia. Having practised and taught for many years in Tokyo, Heneghan has only relatively recently arrived in Australia. He took up the position of chair of architecture at the University of Sydney two years ago. Here, he interviews Leon van Schaik, innovation professor at the Royal Melbourne Institute of Technology (RMIT). Van Schaik has been at RMIT for 17 years, and has had a profound influence on the institute and the city of Melbourne, taking a proactive part in the commissioning of new buildings. He has championed a shift in the culture of education at RMIT, both within the School of Architecture and throughout the institution, in his various roles as professor, dean, pro-vice-chancellor, and now innovation professor of architecture.

Top
Leon van Schaik.

Bottom
Tom Heneghan.

Opposite
Leon van Schaik produced this sketch in preparation for his meeting with Tom Heneghan. Certain inscriptions were added during the talk. It follows a form Leon first established in his diploma project at the AA School of Architecture in 1969/70. A large number of such images were exhibited in the Front Members Room. One of these images appeared on the poster for that show: '75 New Architects'. They were later published by Gillo Dorfles in his book Dal Signifizato Alle Scelte, EINAUDI (Turin), 1973. (cont'd) overleaf

range education we enjoyed at the AA, and which fundamentally shaped so many leading architectural careers. The policies and systems adopted by most universities, internationally, seem to impede creation of the type of educational milieu that so supported those at the AA – especially the institutionalised rhetoric of teaching-and-learning (T&L) policies, in which outcomes have to be prescribed, consequently privileging learning at the expense of discovery.

During the period that Leon and I were students and then unit masters at the AA, staff and students alike pursued self-directed discovery. All were passionate about their domain, and outcomes went beyond any

context of my university is very different from RMIT, our architecture programme is evolving along a different path. It's a long-haul process. Few universities, certainly not sandstone universities, are nimble on their feet.

In our discussion, Leon and I began by revisiting the theoretical basis of our AA experience, which Leon sketched as a mind map. I pressed him to describe how he managed to navigate a passage of similar ideas through the Australian tertiary education accountability framework.

The Beginning: Deciding On the Knowledge Base
Leon van Schaik: A huge division exists over the nature of architecture, which stems from the professionalisation process of the 1830s. An enormous amount still gets done in education, which is driven by

(cont'd from p 33)
The basic form is that of a shoe-box theatre. Curtains can be seen to the left and to the right, and a drop with three downward points links them across the top. This drop presents the enduring condition of our situation, our 'human capabilities' and the ways in which these unfold in space and link us through discoveries united in the 'morphic resonances' of a universe that is a learning system.

The left-hand curtain indicates the 'natural history of the creative individual', while the right-hand curtain is about the 'ritual behaviours that support or constrain creativity'. A sketchy profile on the curtain alludes to the power of mentors such as Peter Cook (pluralist determinist), Alvin Boyarsky (nonclassicising), Kenneth Frampton (classicising) and Aurelio Galfetti (put in the position ...). Some informing canons are listed: formalist Reyner Banham's Well-Tempered Environment;[*] architecture as a custodian of the embedded spatial intelligences of society ...

Added below these during our conversation are some comments pointing to the continuing importance of independent architecture schools like SCI-ARCH; and the leadership of people like Eric Owen Moss through such institutions (Rotundi and Denari might have been mentioned.) The danger of such leadership, 'closing down options', is labelled. We had a feeling that the AA had moved in that direction since the 1970s.

On the stage is a feedback loop labelled 'ENVIRONMENT'. Three positions are floated around this with their attributes dangling below them: professionalisation – dead end, conformity, convergence, conflict of interest; research-based practice – peer-review, Archilab, diversity and divergence;
(cont'd opposite)

those early ambitions to be a profession. In my view, these are mostly misguided. The professional paradigm refers to a group of practitioners who possess an exclusive body of knowledge and exercise it to the good of society. In return for their help, they gain some autonomy. Now, it has never been evident that architecture professionalised on a knowledge base that was in any sense exclusive. That is partly because, despite WR Lethaby (whose book titles and lectures pointed the other way),[1] the power brokers over time chose a technology stream based on the master-builder paradigm, which emphasised the managerial role of architects. All sorts of other people, of course, lay claim to that territory – and quite rightly so.

There is another approach to the knowledge base, and this was the one we adopted at the AA. It is why we are interested in architecture. It is where you and I come in on the same stream. We're interested in it because it is about the unfolding of human capabilities in space. These capabilities are in every human being – they've evolved, and they operate in all sorts of marvellous ways. But for most people they've become totally embedded in unselfconscious things, and they thus disappear from everyday consciousness. I see architecture as something that has a custodial role, looking after human knowledge of spatiality. The role – when it works – puts people back in touch with that knowledge and that experience, so that they begin again to understand how unspoken experiences improve their lives.

There is a big divide between these two approaches in education, because if you go down the technocratic path you're heading towards more and more prescription: to defining curriculum and to defining competencies. On the other path you have to adopt a totally different character – considering architects as psychologists, sociologists and people who study spatial intelligence. Howard Gardner talks about the different kinds of intelligence – logico

mathematical, musical, kinetic, inter- and intrapersonal.[2] Recently he has added naturalist intelligence. Of course architecture uses all of these, but spatial intelligence and its evolution must be at its core – or so many of us believed, and still do.

At the AA we operated within a technocratic professional frame that, on the face of it, was antithetical to these goals, but it was seldom impossible to argue architects around to understanding and supporting it could be otherwise. Nevertheless, we behaved as if the days of the profession were over, and indeed we lived through the ending of the postwar reconstruction social compact as the oil prices soared in the 1970s. What we then experienced was an art-based rebellion – but it was still using the old professional paradigm. What we see emerging now in the profession is a research-based practice, where there is a real divergence – a real difference between people – and little agreement about the nature of the professional. Clients are won through their own research interests, so there is a strong divergence. What was great about the AA was that the school tried to find the unique contribution in everyone, rather than to mould them to some prescribed outcome.

This, too, is what I've been trying to do at RMIT. I've also begun to understand the difference between mastery and creative innovation.[3] This plays out in the same research-based arena. Peter Cook was an important figure in this shift. He introduced pluralism, even if it was a strangely deterministic pluralism. Anything went, as long as it looked up-to-the-minute. At the beginning of the period at the AA, Ken Frampton and Alvin Boyarsky had that famous clash where Frampton basically stood up and said that architecture was solved. All that had to be done now was to frame up the curriculum to this end and put everybody through it so that they could become good Modernists. No need for any more experimentation. We're having no more experimentation! Boyarsky said the opposite: we've only just begun, we don't know what architecture is, where it might go. There can therefore be no curriculum system!

Putting Us in the Position of the Architect

Aurelio Galfetti, who started the architecture school in Mendrisio, in southern Switzerland, came to us at RMIT. In a seminar he proudly stated that in this neophyte age the average age of his staff was 70! He was a great pluralist in that, simultaneously, he would have a studio run by Ken Frampton and one by Peter Zumthor. (It was very funny going into those studios at the end of term and seeing one studio absolutely full of white cardboard models and another absolutely full of brown wooden models.) He said the most wonderful thing when I asked him whether he regarded it as his responsibility to make every student who came though his school into a good architect. He said: 'Well, nobody can do that; all you can do is aim to put the student in the position of being an architect – that could play either way.' And that is what we did, and do. There is a world of difference between 'knowing' what an architect is, and looking for every individual's research passion.

Ritual Behaviours

It is ritual behaviours that either support or constrain people, allowing or preventing them from transcending mastery and becoming creative innovators. Most of what happens at institutions of architecture is about constraining. The groups that form to support creative innovation tend to be informal and short-lived. Most institutionally run conferences are based on the normative profession-paradigm, and though they are supportive to some people they are destructively limiting to others. Surveying the current scene one can see that specialist conferences are very important to certain groups. Archilab is much more open to explorative work that is environmentally radical, for example, and actively promotes a research-based practice paradigm.

Tom Heneghan: **It was the structure of the AA under Boyarsky that enabled creativity to be nurtured rather than confined. The divergent learning environments, known within the school as 'units', were in our time identified not only by number, but also by official or unofficial names – such as 'The Nice Ideas Unit', 'The Urban Politics Unit', 'The Housing Unit'. We didn't at the time label them 'research units' because it seemed entirely** obvious to us that design must result from, and be part of, an investigation of ideas, issues, facts and data. In other words, that design must result from self-selected research.

It is surprising to me that other schools have allowed the separation of research and design – as if design is merely shape-giving or problem-solving, and as if architecture merely involves the application of learned professional skills. It is a misunderstanding of the nature and purpose of creativity throughout history, which has always existed not merely as a need for originality but as a response to issues, and as an investigative step into the dark. To experiment, to judge the result and to step again. To leave prescribed 'learning outcomes' in the dust. The result of all these different experimental units pursuing their different studies, in public, in the same building, was to allow cross-flow, unexpected overlaps and confrontations. These challenged and moved the work on in quantum leaps – all of it was brought into the wider public arena by publications and by exhibiting at the end of the year.

Canons and Other Frames

LVS: One of the chief things we did at the AA was get the students to know and learn from each other. They're always going to learn more from each other than from anybody else – that is built into the natural history of creative people. What is currently happening to universities is causing increasing convergence in the learning experience. This is because of the way universities react to government policies – they all seem to move in the same direction, which is an utter disaster if you agree with our passion-based, research-led model, in which it is sometimes hard to tell who is the tutor and who is the student!

The issue of canons and other frames comes to my mind – the 'performance' canons you refer to, the 'well-tempered environment' canon and the 'architects without architecture' canon. If you shift the basis of education from the profession paradigm to the research paradigm, then in a sense this is about exploring the embedded custodial role of the practice of architecture. Somewhere in that custodial role those different canons can be reconciled. At the AA, and now, I framed this all up within a belief that the universe is a learning system. I believe in 'morphic resonance': that ideas tend to emerge all over the place at about the same time. Sheldrake[4] argues that there's a huge amount of evidence to support this. It shifts the focus away from originality and into our shared human capabilities, and helps society maintain an awareness of them and their uses through each architect unfolding and developing his or her spatial intelligence.

Since being in Australia, thanks to Ruth Dunkin I have learned of another framework that supports what

[cont'd from p 34]
platforms of mastery – creative innovation, diversity, divergence and competition.

The stage is fronted by a row of footlights. Below these are listed the four integrated scholarships of the Boyer model: Discovery, Integration, Application and Dissemination.[8]

In the audience space sits a 'mental map' bubble: Innovation is creative originality subjected to sustained attention. An overlapped bubble lists Alvin Boyarsky's leadership at its best: generosity being defined as 'whatever decision you make, make sure it opens up more options'. These words come from Heinz von Foerster through Ranulph Glanville. WH Auden's 'choose the odd' might have been located here too.

Below this is a reference to the changing learning environments that are emerging through the Internet, and below that are some of the 19th-century control mechanisms that bedevil education today: credit-point systems, and the notion that one should teach to specified outcomes. These comments were added as we spoke.

'What is currently happening to universities is causing increasing convergence in the learning experience. This is because of the way universities react to government policies – they all seem to move in the same direction, which is an utter disaster if you agree with our passion-based, research-led model, in which it is sometimes hard to tell who is the tutor and who is the student!'

we were trying to do, and still do, and this is the Boyer Scholarship Model, which comes out of the US through the Carnegie Education Institute.[5] Boyer led a reappraisal of the role of the professoriate in the university. The team grappled with the apparent conflicting demands of teaching and research as they surface in most academic institutions (though not our AA!), and in a wonderfully architectural way they found a holistic reconciliation. They proposed that in a healthy professoriate everyone is engaged in scholarship, be it discovering new knowledge ('pure research'), or integrating new findings into existing knowledge, or applying new knowledge to existing problems, or disseminating knowledge through teaching and other forms of communication. When they looked at the different forms of scholarship they came to the conclusion that they all relied on the same mechanisms for evaluating quality – peer review of a nature appropriate to the practice. When an institution understands this, it takes away much of the disruptive energy that exists in universities where people are fighting for one or another of these approaches at the expense of the others. Often within their own lives! When scholarship is the focus, then people are beginning to actually see that if things are framed appropriately, then everything done is usable by everybody else.

If you think back to the system at the AA, that was what we did. Everyone of us had to frame up his or her research direction for the year and present it to the student body, who would then choose which research path they wanted to follow. During the year there were crits by outsiders that focused on our research and its progress through the work of the individual students. We were all on the line together. And then at the end of the year there was a public presentation of the work to everyone after the externally examined reviews of the work of each of our units. The discussions were as much about what we had been trying to explore as they were about individual progress. I think integrated scholarship is one of the most helpful things we've come across at RMIT, and it's dramatically helped us to deal with the seriously difficult situation schools face in these times.

TH: **One of the difficulties is the perception that architecture is a visual and professional pursuit rather than an academic one in which ideas are interrogated. But, while some academics increasingly understand that design can be seen as a legitimate form of research, it is not easy to locate it within the regular structure of academic research, nor to frame it in a way that traditional researchers recognise as research.**

'Architecture is in a very difficult position in the more traditional universities because of all sorts of suspicions held by other disciplines about the nature of scholarship and architecture. At RMIT we've been working at establishing a distinctive research culture for 15 years, based on the integrated scholarship model, which is very much the secret.'

LVS: Architecture is in a very difficult position in the more traditional universities because of all sorts of suspicions held by other disciplines about the nature of scholarship and architecture. At RMIT we've been working at establishing a distinctive research culture for 15 years, based on the integrated scholarship model, which is very much the secret. But what is being described as inhibiting research is very interesting.

TH: **A large question is: how to deal with the professional demands on universities? At the AA, people like James Stirling, Richard Rogers and David Alford, of YRM, who were our external examiners, were eager to enter into debates and learn from student and unit experiments. Here in Australia, although at the University of Sydney we have had very pleasing support from the Visiting Board of the Royal Australian Institute of Architects for the intellectual content of our design programmes, there are many professionals who seem to think our experiments are peripheral.**

With starting salaries of AUS$35,000 mandated by the Australian government, prospective employers argue that new staff must be immediately operational in all roles, with comprehensive knowledge of practice law. At the AA we thought, 'Well, there really is too much to talk about' to deal with that too, and it was dealt with later, in the early stages of practice in the British articled way. We saw the time at the AA as a time of development. In Australia, it seems university courses are viewed as a time of completion, and this colours the students' views of the purpose of the course. Many feel that they must concentrate on being employable, and some seem little interested in the quality of their university design work because they know that it won't affect their ability to get a job in Australia's booming economy. I wonder whether architecture as we talk of it can be taught in this framework.

Part of what made the AA was that the students self-selected their route through their education. This relied

on a pretty motivated student body, and we selected from the applicants on the basis of their motivation and aptitude, not on their high-school exam results. The students who come into the university system here in Australia would not necessarily get into the AA. In fact many would never consider applying to the AA. They would not think it was sufficiently prestigious.

In Tokyo there are two major national architecture schools, both of which you can only get into if you are academically extraordinary. At the masters level, Tokyo University is unparalleled, but at the undergraduate level it is Tokyo National University of Arts that has the outstanding programme, and this difference is essentially created by the student intake. Students who are keen for security, success and who plan to eventually take leading positions in government join the undergraduate course at Tokyo University. But, those who are more interested in architecture as a culture, and aim to run their own 'ateliers', tend to go to Tokyo National University of Arts – where I taught for a number of years.

Annual intake at Tokyo University is 60 to 80 students. Annual intake at Tokyo National University is 14 to 16. Students often repeat the entrance exams for more than three years in order to win their place in that 14. By their determination and focus they self-select. They are prepared to seek out the most critical environment. Here, many of the students are seeing their entrée to a professional career as their outcome, not the commencement of a life-long engagement with learning.

LVS: What's being described is precisely how the architecture programme at the University of Newcastle on Tyne was run in the 1960s, down to the point that the final two years were actually run as a pseudo office. So I don't think it is a regional thing; it is a mindset that exists in the UK, the US and elsewhere. It is one that a school can be very readily dominated by if it does not have a larger theoretical frame from which to construct its approach. It is tied to this old-fashioned but still very powerful notion of architecture as a profession.

RMIT has always had a part-time mode, which runs alongside the full-time programme; there is a single five-year bachelor of architecture degree that runs in conjunction with part-time courses. The main reason for all of this is that our students are in and out of work all the way through their learning careers. Recent research shows that this is the case for most students in Australia. We try to make use of that

consciously: weaving between work and study makes students less susceptible to theory shock. I noticed in England that often the first three years of a programme in provincial schools are quite lively, and then students would go out into the offices and go, 'Oh my God'. They would come back totally disillusioned with everything that they'd learned at school with any enjoyment; they would say: 'None of it is relevant in the office system.'

That doesn't happen at RMIT. The students move between the most abstruse theoretical positions and working in somebody's office on a daily basis. They learn how to apply theory in the office, and I'm sure that's one of the secrets. The other one is the complete integration of practitioners into the school at RMIT. The AA and RMIT have always been places where practitioners do their research – their creative research. It's a two-way thing. In the traditional universities, many of the students are there not because they want to be architects but because they haven't got into law or medicine, and for some reason in these universities architecture is under enormous pressure from the profession to produce people with certain managerial capabilities, because they are destined to be leaders. In reality the graduates of the AA, then, and RMIT, now, have those capabilities and it's partly because they have 'street cred' that they go into architecture. They fight to get in. Very often they've already tried law or medicine and thought 'It's just not for me'. Once they've decided what they want to do they come to us.

As to students' choice of school, once again we need an overarching frame, so that the choices that people make are understandable. If you look at the natural history of creative individuals, they're almost always driven to be on the edge, because their interests take them that way. They're always suspicious of establishment situations. There is a lot of profiling that's been done by people like Theodor Zelden and Howard Gardner, among others, who have studied

'What's being described is precisely how the architecture programme at the University of Newcastle on Tyne was run in the 1960s, down to the point that the final two years were actually run as a pseudo office. So I don't think it is a regional thing; it is a mindset that exists in the UK, the US and elsewhere.'

'T&L theorists seem to have convinced themselves that students must be taught architecture as a sequence of very prescribed, graded steps, in which all the students of a given year are taught the same thing at the same time, discuss the same thing at the same time, and design the same thing at the same time. My view is that this is a method of training, rather than of education, since it reduces the student to a receiver, rather than a participant in a culture, and it falsely implies that architecture is not a discipline in which it is appropriate to pursue research-led learning.'

intentions – to identify effective ways of imparting an education – but it has been accused of standardising mediocrity and of proscribing experiment, and consequently advance, in education. The requirement for clearly predicted outcomes is a particular issue. The nature of experiment is that there can be no clearly predicted outcomes. T&L theorists seem to have convinced themselves that students must be taught architecture as a sequence of very prescribed, graded steps, in which all the students of a given year are taught the same thing at the same time, discuss the same thing at the same time, and design the same thing at the same time. My view is that this is a method of training, rather than of education, since it reduces the student to a receiver, rather than a participant in a culture, and it falsely implies that architecture is not a discipline in which it is appropriate to pursue research-led learning.

In addition to this, credit-points systems drain the life out of the educational experience by mistakenly equating time spent with knowledge learned, and by reducing education to a score. Students have told me that they are not interested in exploring any learning opportunity that does not earn them credit points.

LVS: One of the most insidious things that has happened is the modularisation of the curriculum and the allocation of credit points to each unit of learning. It is something that appears to place a quantifiable value on each unit of learning. It also requires administrators to believe that a curriculum can be devised to cover the entire territory. It ties back to the TAFEs (teaching and further education colleges) and competencies, when in fact the most important outcome for architectural education is that the staff are totally dumbfounded by what the students have done and are left grappling with how to assess it! Valuing that it is different to what they've experienced before, as opposed to having to describe how it's going to be assessed and previously describing what the learning outcome is. The learning outcome is going to be different for everyone. The other thing the credit-points system implies is that there is a logical pathway through the area. It doesn't matter where you begin, as long as it is driven by curiosity. We haven't been able to completely surmount that at RMIT. We try to attract anyone passing by, as we did at the AA, asking them to come in and give a lecture. We have had to do all sorts of contorted things like the 'Dean's lecture series': you sign on for it at the beginning of the semester, you don't know what it is; it's got so many credit points, and at the end of term you submit a diary of the events you have attended and digested!

I did this because I began to be the most seriously well-educated person in the entire school. I was at every lecture and there were only a handful of other people there because it wasn't part of the curriculum. I found that really destructive when I first started.

people who have made a creative contribution to their discipline area. You don't just find them getting there by being at the most prestigious institution – that's not the driver.

I was at Harvard as a visiting fellow for a semester in 1994 and, although it was then under Mack Scogin's leadership, Raphael Moneo's influence was enormously powerful still. I had a student there who was taking the logic of everything he was doing and was ending up with a very pointy design. He burst into tears (this was a mature student!). I said: 'What's the matter?' He said: 'Well, anything that shape will fail because it just doesn't fit into what I know passes here, and if I don't change this to look like that other stuff I'll have lost $60,000 this year!' There was a very good argument; it was an extremely compelling argument for what he was doing with his project. We could see that. It was, however, conflicting with what he believed to be the outcomes that were necessary in order to get the Harvard degree. As it was, I persuaded him to carry on and I think he got the year prize for his design. Choice of school is an interesting tension that I don't think is only an Australian problem, or a problem in the US. There, too, you'll get people who deliberately choose to go to SCI-ARCH as opposed to any of the Ivy League universities, and they'll be certain kinds of people. The pity is that those who opt for prestige opt for a mastery that inhibits innovation.

TH: The teaching-and-learning machine in Australia seems to be more institutionalised than in England. Obviously, it springs from good

The existing T&L model is very strange. It is going to be completely shot out of the water by the Internet, as it develops and as people begin to use it fully. Why should they wait for an institution to serve up teaching? If they've got any gumption at all they won't be waiting for this trickle-down of teaching from a timetable devised to suit administration rather than their learning needs. At RMIT I've tried to tackle the tyranny of the curriculum-based timetable, in which there is a lecture on professional practice once a week and a lecture on history once a week. So that every week there is a lecture on something across the smorgasbord of what you're supposed to know – as if what you're supposed to know could be covered by a timetable! As if any domain can be covered in a curriculum.

In a university there's endless pressure to add more subjects because various literacies are seen to be crucial: 'What about occupational health and safety? What about indigeneity?' It just goes on and on. It never stops. The thing that then happens is that the student experience becomes this really grey thing, and so does the staff experience; all semester, week by week the staff are giving down this little bit of information and the student lives in a haze of information in drifting modules. What should be happening, as it did at the AA, and now does at RMIT as well as in more enlightened schools of engineering – none of which are in Australia – is that you actually get as much of the lecturing stuff done in conference mode upfront. You can then devote the rest of the semester to research, which is

project based, and at the end produce conclusions and designs. Assessments are then based on performance in terms of various literacies. This does two things: it means that staff can actually construct a conference in which the overarching frame is well interrogated, and that we can have the best speakers available. For the rest of the semester students can free themselves up to do research and practice.

Even when students who are 'digital natives' realise they can do without the restrictive practices of universities, they will still need to get together with people who are interesting. At RMIT, students participate in the experiments of really very interesting people, who are expressly engaged in scholarship in their own right, not as servants to a curriculum. At most universities, when they use practitioners a full-time academic staff has set a project for a year of students and the practitioners come in and crit what the students are doing on a set project. At RMIT, if you're teaching, we ask you to set the project, so it's like having units at the AA, and the project has to be one that is of theoretical concern to you and that is extending your knowledge base.

People like Kerstin Thompson have used years of studio teaching to actually extend the whole notion of what the surface means to architecture, working with dedicated groups of students who come from a range of different levels of experience in the course. So have many others: Carey Lyon, Peter Elliott, Howard Raggatt, Ian Macdougall. Now a much younger generation are involved (and those I've named used to be young once, too, I might point out!). They're all there, not running something where it's been decided that everyone will do a nursery school. Students pick their own pathway through. I currently have a nephew studying architecture at RMIT. At some distance I can observe how he has moved through the programme, picking his way through, his parents watching from overseas. At the beginning he was wondering what was interesting and slowly gaining confidence. Then he was purposefully creating an educational pathway for himself. This is what you have to do at RMIT. No two students will graduate from RMIT along the same pathway.

TH: **But at RMIT your rejection of curriculum and year structure goes beyond even what was occurring at the AA, with no division between years.**

LVS: At RMIT there is a distinction between upper pool and lower pools so there is an informal clustering in the school, but people can negotiate themselves up and down. I think that's another absolutely crucial symbol of our overarching educational model. I believed in this strongly at the AA and here. You learn more from other students than from anyone else and you learn more from students who have some experience. So the mix in one group is a learning accelerator. Critics become very rapidly aware of what's going on in assessment and

'Assessments are then based on performance in terms of various literacies. This does two things: it means that staff can actually construct a conference in which the overarching frame is well interrogated, and that we can have the best speakers available. For the rest of the semester students can free themselves up to do research and practice.'

'To succeed you have to get involved in management. I have also spent a lot of time working across the university trying to get people to understand the integrated (Boyer) scholarship model. Engineering is trying to move in this direction. It goes very slowly, but there is quite a big base at RMIT.'

they ask, 'What level are you in?', and then try to judge what you're doing and your level of judgement against an appropriate level of experience, so it works. It was part of the culture when I came – under the custodial care of Peter Downton, who has been an unfailing advocate and ally. With the university it was a battle in the beginning, and some staff went to extraordinary lengths to sabotage what we had done. The strategy has always been to be ahead in conceptualising and articulating what we are doing, so that as new systems roll out, we can say: 'Oh that? We do that this way!' The current leadership in architecture are very adept at that, I am proud to say.

The approach of the University of Newcastle, in Australia, which is said to be problem based, is also a step in the right direction. Though I am suspicious of the way they do it stepwise. I don't agree with starting with a kiosk, then a simple little house and then a branch library and then a nursery school and so on, until you reach a hospital. This is a deterministic approach that removes most exploration from architecture, boiling it down to a mastering of building types. I think this is again part of the misreading of Piaget that Gardner's research has revealed. Piaget identified the different modes of learning but when he argued that they unfold one after the other in a developmental sequence he was reading his data through a progress model that his research did not support. It is now clear that all of the categories of awareness that he described coexist and unfold according to the opportunities that are presented, not in some preordained stage-by-stage developmental process. The curriculum approach is based on such progression models.

TH: The transformation of RMIT from a second-tier institution into an agenda-setting, internationally respected architecture programme has been quite remarkable. Your 'Masters by Invitation' programme has had a considerable effect on the work of the many exceptionally talented practitioners who have joined the course as students. You've moved RMIT into the public domain through publications on the school's research, through exhibitions, and through the new, controversial building by Ashton Raggatt McDougal, which you commissioned to house it.

LVS: In the early days there were a lot of credit-point chasers. There are, however, ways in which to build ambition in the student group. One of them is capturing the knowledge that they generate. When I arrived at RMIT there was an end-of-year pin-up, but there was no such thing as an exhibition. The pin-up happens widely in Australia, but the kind of efforts that would go into making an exhibition are mostly avoided. There was nothing like the end-of-year show as happened at the AA. So in fact, in 1986 I set the senior students the challenge and we started in 1987 with the 'Major Projects Review'. It has been running ever since. These are public exhibitions, to a very high standard, of the best of the major projects. There is a catalogue that is also that generation's own manifesto. Sometimes it's been every year, but now it is every two years. It tends to be in April and it's in a public venue – everyone in the profession comes and looks at it. There is a prize awarded, which is a memorial prize to a young architect who died in a horse-riding accident, as well as a publication. The publication part is very important too. Now I know there's enormous competition amongst the students to get into that exhibition. It's a post-graduation exhibition and it runs outside the pin-up season, which still happens at the end of the year. It has certainly galvanised ambition.

Other things have also worked to build student ambition, like Transition, and the various publications that come out under Harriet Edquist's leadership. The level of ambition at RMIT is now much higher than it was when I first arrived, when there was a very different culture.

TH: One of the reasons you seem to have been able to achieve so much is that you have been prepared to get embroiled in your university's management structure, as professor, then as dean, then as pro-vice-chancellor.

LVS: To succeed you have to get involved in management. I have also spent a lot of time working across the university trying to get people to understand the integrated (Boyer) scholarship model. Engineering is trying to move in this direction. It goes very slowly, but there is quite a big base at RMIT. Art Design and Communications have taken to it fairly readily because there is something in their tradition that relates to it. Fashion has also just come into the School of Architecture and Design because it is seeking the intellectual framework of integrated scholarship. You do need to describe what you're doing so that you can demonstrate that you are accountable. One of the responsibilities of scholarship is that you actually do have an awareness of what you're doing, that you can describe the experiment/project you are engaged in and assess its success or otherwise, so that you can describe how your findings touch other domains, and can describe it in such a way that it can be peer-reviewed. This work needs to be done, but it is not extra work. It's a smart shift – doing what you do differently and more effectively.

At the AA there was a process that is exactly like the scholarship model, because at the beginning of the year you stood up in front of a crowd of people, you said this is my theoretical field and this is what we're going to study. Then at the end of the year you would have an exhibition at which you demonstrated whether what you'd done stood up to scrutiny or not. You had a one-year contract, and if it didn't stand up to scrutiny you were out. That horrifies people in Australia. But Peter Cook had 25 years of one-year contracts, and he is one of the most influential educators of the century. It was an extreme kind of model but it did do what was necessary to develop everyone as 'scholars' – people in possession of their research questions, and able to pursue these in practice, whether they were staff or students. Then at the end you demonstrate your outcomes, and it's in the public forum.

One of the things that astounded me at RMIT when I started was that there was no external assessment. This is impossible: you have to have people from outside, or there is no credible review process. When I enquired into it, I understood that Australia had actually adopted a Scottish model that was very strongly organised around the presumed professionalism of the teacher. No one dared interfere with that – 'the teacher knows and the teacher assesses'. It was a big battle. There was an enquiry into it, but I introduced external moderation. Without that, there is no scholarship.

Currently people think that what we're trying to do is doomed by the Nelson report,[6] but I think the young staff understand this Boyer scholarship so well that they can ride over the

top of this new policy wave. But I could not have done this alone. To do it as a sole person in the university system? I don't see how you can do it; the whole group have to adopt a mental map of what it's about. But there are ways of moving, even with a strong, established staff complement and a timetable system, if the players understand the model. What I've tried to do is to get every member of staff to be a scholar in his or her own right, and only be doing what develops his or her scholarship. In the end, the students are going to go to places because of the reputations of the scholars there.

TH: People talk a lot about the AA's influence on themselves, and also on the development of the architecture programmes at the world's leading schools. What I think has been done at RMIT is to extend and renew that paradigm. In the 1970s, described as architectural experimentation, it's now identified as research done through design in a scholarly manner. And, by identifying that, it's given it a purpose and focus and meaning as part of our collective investigations into the nature and culture of architecture. In this way it's erased the gap between those who 'do' architecture, and those who discuss it; between the practitioner and the academic. The proposition is that all work in architecture, whether practical or academic, can be assessed as scholarly enquiry, and the scholarly application of knowledge provokes a distinct change in our perceptions of our work and of architectural education.

LVS: I have always agreed with Alvin Boyarsky when he is reputed to have said on his deathbed: 'There will be no curriculum system at the AA!' The curriculum system seems to deny the nature of the university, the learning system – it denies everything that we know about.

TH: It is arguable that architecture, which engages both in practice and in education with changes in so many of the humanities and sciences, is consequently subject to more rapid and more thorough changes than any other discipline. And, as the nature of architecture changes, the nature of architectural education must change correspondingly. The question is whether the ways of institutionalised higher learning are compatible with such change, and whether the universities' lack of agility explains the predominance in architectural education of independent architecture schools such as the AA, SCI-ARCH, the Berlage Institute, Stadelschule, the Cranbrook Institute, the semi-independent Harvard GSD, etc. The achievements of 'pluralist dictators' such as Peter Cook at the UCL Bartlett, Bernard Tschumi at Columbia and Leon van Schaik at RMIT – all themselves products of Alvin Boyarsky's pluralist dictatorship at the AA – are the exceptions at the larger institutions, and in this discrepancy the challenge to architectural education is laid bare. ∆

Notes
1 WR Lethaby, Architecture, Nature & Magic, Gerald Chatsworth & Co (London), 1956.
2 Howard Gardner, Intelligence Reframed: Multiple Intelligences for the 21st Century, Basic Books (New York), 1999.
3 Van Schaik is publishing a book on the subject of mastery and creative innovation with Wiley-Academy in the autumn of 2005.
4 Rupert Sheldrake, 'The rebirth of nature', in Pavel Buchler and Nikos Papastergiadis (eds), Random Access 2: Ambient Fears, Rivers Oram (London), pp 100–121; also Rupert Sheldrake, The Sense of Being Stared At, and Other Aspects of the Extended Mind, Hutchinson (London), 2003.
5 Ernest L Boyer, Scholarship Reconsidered: Priorities of the Professoriate, The Carnegie Foundation for the Advancement of Teaching (Princeton, NJ), 1990.
6 The Nelson report is a Federal Government White Paper on university education, named for the current Australian Federal Minister for Education. It proposes a tightening of curriculum specification, amongst other so-called accountability measures.
7 Reyner Banham, The Architecture of the Well-Tempered Environment, The Architectural Press (London), 1973.
8 Boyer, op cit.

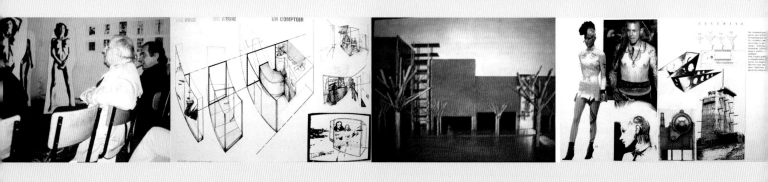

Paul Virilio

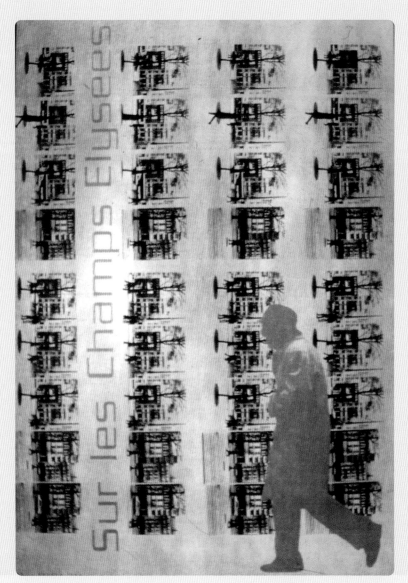

Sur les Champs Elysées

The influential cultural theorist, Paul Virilio, has had an intensive and extensive career in architectural education in France. **Charles Bessard**, a former student of his at the Ecole Spéciale d'Architecture, describes this previously undiscussed aspect of Virilio's work, interviewing Virilio on his views on schools today and how they relate to his recent philosophical treatises.

To most people, Paul Virilio is a cultural theorist and an essayist with a special focus on the implications of technologies – in speed and war, as well as in the media – on the politics and organisation of space. Many of his books are considered the most pre-eminent and controversial writings on the technocultural transformations of our contemporary environment. Among these are: The Aesthetics of Disappearance; Speed and Politics; Negative Horizon: Toward a Dromoscopy; L'insécurité du territoire; Art and Fear; and Unknown Quantity. However, for around 2,000 people Paul Virilio was first of all their teacher in architecture. For more than 30 years, between 1968 and 1999, not only was he an emeritus professor in architecture at the Ecole Spéciale d'Architecture (ESA) in Paris; he also became chairman and director of the same institution.

Surprisingly – and despite his considerable commitment to teaching activities – this area of Virilio's

work remains very much unknown. Virilio himself speaks very little of his experience as a teacher, so any trace of his intensive educational career is scattered only in the memories of his students. Twelve years after I had been a part of his unit, I went to La Rochelle to interview him, to discuss the views he has developed throughout his many years of teaching. How does he relate his writings to his role as a teacher? How did his approach to teaching evolve from the turmoil of the events of May 1968[1] to the ideological void of today? How does he elaborate his teaching methods? What and how to teach architecture today? What is the impact of new technologies on architectural education and what it produces?

Two hours of interrogation revealed a hidden side of Virilio's multifaceted profile and a controversial vision of today's architectural education and practice.

In fact, the reason why this side of Virilio's work has remained unknown lies very much in its essence. He admits to having kept a few documents to write a short piece on education, but the intensity and frequency of catastrophic global events of recent years, collected in his book Unknown Quantities and which confirmed his philosophical approach, have prevented him writing the piece.

A further reason why so few of his documents can be found today is because his teaching was based mainly on the oral media. Of course, as a writer he circulated numerous books around the unit, but certainly – and voluntarily – not his own. Thus the main activity of the studio consisted of intense dialogues between Virilio and his students, and as a result: '**All has vanished of this period and all that is left is you my students! And I am glad about that.**'

Although Virilio is a theoretician, he never theorised his teaching further than purposefully restricting it to a dialogue and contact with the other. He never taught us his architectural theories. For him, architects who teach what they write commit themselves to reproducing the mistake of the academic education of the Beaux-Arts. Although Architecture Principe, the office funded by Virilio and Claude Parent, had a radical and controversial viewpoint, Virilio didn't get involved in the education environment to preach this. Rather the opposite.

After five years of architectural practice, between 1963 and 1968, and three projects

(Thompson factory, Mariotti's house and the Sainte Bernadette du Banlay Church), the practice experienced a critical period, lacking any new commissions. This economic crisis threatened the existence of the practice and the association between its two partners. However, it was history that consummated the divorce between the pair, by revealing a deep ideological disagreement. As the events of May 1968 burst on to the streets, Claude Parent joined the right wing in condemning the insurrection, whereas Virilio went left, supporting the students and committing to their actions. It was these circumstances which, a few months later, led the students of the ESA to call for Virilio to teach architecture.

So it was in the turmoil of the 1968 revolution that Virilio entered the ESA. Students from universities all over France went on to the streets to condemn the traditional dogmatic and passive educational system that relied on the study of manuals, and which channelled them through rigid and predefined courses with no opportunity to make cross-disciplinary shifts.

Very quickly the condemnation spread to a general rejection of the paternalism and determinism of the postwar welfare state and its rigid Establishment, as well as a rejection of the consumer society and its afferent capitalist system. Slogans such as 'Power to imagination', 'Dream is reality', 'Let's be realistic, claim the impossible', 'It is forbidden to forbid' or 'Run comrade, the old world is behind you' covered walls all over France.

At the ESA, students immediately dismantled the classical educational system; they rejected the legitimacy of tutors as student censors, sacked the old professors and claimed management of the school. The May 1968 events had a particularly strong influence on the ESA because as the only private school of architecture in France its educational programme did not have to bear the yoke of the ministry, and it therefore afforded the opportunity to experiment with new educational schemes and theories.

Virilio saw these events as a double opportunity. First, they provided the chance to focus on the theoretical works he engaged in after the failure of his building activities. And second, they opened up the way to establishing what was, for him, a new kind of relationship with the 'concrete world', through his contact with the students – a contact with the 'other'. This relationship to the 'other' developed through the elaboration of pedagogical techniques based on both his interaction with the students and a close monitoring of contemporary events.

'**I am very much grafted to the events that surround me; I think I was an internationalist before the globalisation.**' And this is one of the very rare links he

November 22-December 18
Gallery Hours
Wed.-Sun. 12-6pm
Opening Reception
November 22 7-9pm

STOREFRONT
for Art & Architecture

Project DMZ

International Invited exhibition of theoretical proposals for events, strategies, designs, objects, ideas and other forms of action, situated to take place within the physical or conceptual frame work of the DMZ between North and South Korea. In general, a set of possibilities that could provoke the elimination of the DMZ, the unification of Korea and untangled response by art and architecture, on sociopolitical confrontation.

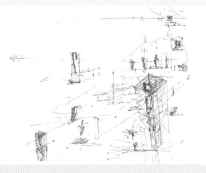

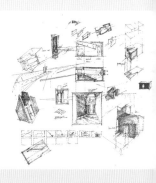

made between his writings and his teaching methods. As a 'war baby', the circumstances of the Second World War have had a deep influence on Virilio's work. With his inductive method of writing, he builds his argument most often on his observations and analysis of a heterogeneous variety of events, from technological discoveries, conflicts and political crises to art exhibitions or celebrity behaviours. In his studio the latest events were frequently discussed, and often reappeared in projects as referential images or quotes propping up the students' proposals.

On joining the ESA in 1968, Virilio instigated, and helped the students establish, a co-management of the school, which became a truly democratic institution directed equally by the students, tutors, managerial and administration staff. In this system, everybody took part in the elaboration of the courses and choice of tutors. All participants had to commit to the debate and become involved in the running of the establishment, which meant total freedom for the students: freedom in choosing the units and the programme, and freedom in the management of the school. This 'free commune' lasted for almost 10 years, before slowly fading away alongside rapid depoliticisation of the students.

However, though the influence of May 1968 on the institutional organisation was waning, Virilio's teaching maintained many of its original characteristics until his last studio in 1999 – for example, his emphasis on the oral over the written word. For him, the notion of dialogue was the essential feature of the relationship between students and tutors.

'Vladimir Jankelevitch made me want to teach because he was teaching like a trapeze artist without any safety net. He used to come into the large auditorium of La Sorbonne and say: "Today we are going to speak about four points", and then he would carry on without any written papers, just a few guidelines – that's all. It dazzled me in the discovery of the oral character. In the oral character there are some things that we discover together. Sometimes it was better than others. Sometimes he would say: "Well it was not so good today; we'll do better next time." That was what really inspired me in my teaching, and without Jankelevitch I would never have taught.'

For Virilio, the idea of dialogue avoids the traditional methods of teaching. The relationship between tutor and students becomes an active partnership: 'The students and I are like sparring partners; it's a partnership, which is radically different from a scheme where one has the knowledge and the other receives it.'

When introducing us to his unit, Virilio warned us that he would teach us nothing, but instead would act as a personal manager. He assumed that the knowledge was already in each of us and that his role was only to reveal it through his pedagogical methods. The responsibility of the tutor and the student was reversed. Students had to bring their position, their personal approach and understanding, before receiving anything, thereby changing in status as they switched from the passive role of receptacles to the active role of authors of the debate.

Virilio would constantly push us to expose ourselves, to adopt points of view, and would force us to make them stronger and more personal. For him there was only one type of architect: author. He would tell the students: 'Author or unemployed – you must choose.' Such statements, in relation to the vast economic crisis in the discipline in the late 1980s, put tremendous pressure on us, his remarks sometimes hitting us literally like punches. Again he compared his unit to a boxing match, in that we would give and ride punches, not to harm but to become stronger and more agile. There was no winner and no loser in this match, and this was perhaps the toughest aspect, because we could never be sure which side we were standing on – that of the author or the unemployed?

Most of the assignments were external competitions, and even when they were not they had to be presented as such. By this means Virilio was pursuing two goals.

The first was to prepare us for our professional lives, because in France substantial parts of contracts are distributed through competitions. This requires a particular way of formatting the work, in which the roles of image and representation are crucial. As a winner of the Grand Prix de la Critique Architectural, Virilio was very often invited on to competition juries, and as his students we benefited greatly from his experienced criticism. This was especially so because, for most competitions, no detailed jury reports are ever produced, and it is therefore impossible to know really why a particular entry has been unsuccessful. I can't remember Virilio making much comment about plans or sections, but I remember he always commented on the renderings with a particular insistence. The representation was of prime importance, and this was obvious in the schedule of the projects. The lap of time for each assignment was divided into three equal periods: generally three weeks for the concept, three weeks for the architecture, three weeks for the presentation.

The second goal was to generate a great diversity of projects. In this respect Virilio completely rejected the traditional education of the Beaux-Arts, where on one side there is the master and on the other the students who copy the master. All of us had to be authors; thus our projects had to be very personal and could only be different.

I remember that Virilio was often criticised by other tutors for his writings and radical conclusions on the effects of technologies on the organisation of space. Thus there was a vague idea that his units would be be about speed and

> I remember that Virilio was often criticised by other tutors for his writings and radical conclusions on the effects of technologies on the organisation of space. Thus there was a vague idea that his units would be about speed and media, and that projects had to be about airports, digital libraries or teleports.

media, and that projects had to be about airports, digital libraries or teleports. But this was definitely not the case and, in fact, when I entered the unit I remember being surprised by the way he was looking at every project with the same enthusiasm. Somehow it seemed that he was more interested in their differences than in their intrinsic value.

The competition format was, for Virilio, a refusal to be considered as a master and a warranty that his students would not be tempted to copy his own work. He consciously never taught us his theories nor the architectural concepts he developed with Architecture Principe. The two main reasons for this were, first, because he didn't believe it would be possible to implement them as such in a building and, second, because he didn't believe in an architecturology. 'Architecture is not an exact science,' therefore there is not one singular and definitive intelligence of architecture, and neither is there

a unique good or bad architecture. It would, of course, be much more banal to claim this today than was the case 30 years ago when Modernism dominated the architectural debate. But Virilio was deeply convinced that diversity in architecture was an absolute necessity.

However, this attitude and démarche raise the question of how it is possible to teach, and criticise projects, without relating to the idea of a good and a bad architecture, and without taking a position?

To escape this dead end, Virilio elaborated an assignment that was central to his teaching: the triptych – an assignment that was carried out individually and at the beginning of the year. The triptych is based upon the idea of a 'pedagogy of value', where it is not the teacher who bestows the value but the opposite: the value is found by the student. In fact, the triptych is not actually an assignment but a method used in the architectural project process. Virilio introduced it in the following terms:

'Usually a project starts with a sketch – the sign is plus, it's a good sketch selected among others. Then there is the scheme design, and the sign of value is still plus – it's a good scheme design. And, finally, there is the final project, and the sign of value is still plus. That is what I call making the value stutter. In my pedagogy of value we do not do that. We start with a bad project, so the sign of value is minus. Then we do a good project, and the sign is plus. And, finally, we do the project beyond, and the sign is multiplied. This means that the value does not stutter – it is produced by what precedes it.'

The three projects described above were carried out on the same programme, site and budget. The first two would last usually two to three weeks each, and the last around a month.

The bad project, which was the most difficult, had to be taken seriously; it could not be bad to the point of being ridiculous – it had to be buildable. In summary, it had to be bad in respect to the brief, the site and the budget. And it had to be bad in a way that someone other than the author could eventually like it. As we proceeded with the bad projects we had to discuss with Virilio and the other students why a particular project was bad. And while we were criticising our own projects we had to prepare what would be the good project. Then, while we were working on the good project, we had to be thinking about the project beyond. Each of these phases was subject to intense debates about what one would consider good or bad, but each time it was the student who proposed the value, and certainly not the teacher. The three projects were displayed together at the end, allowing the student to visualise whether or not the leap forward was successful. With this approach, the value does not exist as

PLAYROOM

FORECAST

MISSION 66

Beatriz Colomina

as follows:

(1) We never align ou
chapter title "Pornoto
will not release any m
(2) We only allow up
PORNOTOPIA
multiple images--photo
numbered 4 features fi
(3) We do not release
numbered 3, 5, 13, 16)

Let me know if you wan

The unstinting rise of academicism within architecture schools is a common gripe among educators. Beatriz Colomina places fact against fiction and examines the truth behind the myth by looking at who is teaching what. She discusses what the functions of history, theory and research might be in architecture schools.

COCKPIT

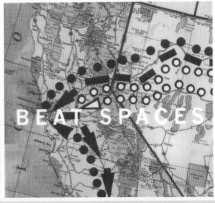

BEAT SPACES

PLASTICS

Opposite

Graphics taken from the cover of the book Cold War Hothouses: Inventing Postwar Culture from Plastics to Playboy, edited by Beatriz Colomina, Ann Marie Brennan and Jeannie Kim, Princeton Architectural Press, 2004. The book, entirely written by PhD candidates, emerged from a series of seminars and workshops on the Cold War, held at Princeton University School of Architecture, by Beatriz Colomina.

Top left

Alcoa aluminium ball gown advertisement, designed by Jean Desses, Paris, and photographed by Richard Avedon, as it appeared in The New Yorker, 13 October 1956. Image from Ann Marie Brennan's article 'Forecast' in Cold War Hothouses.

Top middle

Alcoa aluminium modular shelter, designed by Eliot Noyes and photographed by William Bell, as it appeared in The New Yorker, 25 July 1959. Image from Ann Marie Brennan's article 'Forecast' in Cold War Hothouses.

Top right

Accordion camp trailer designed by Henry Glass and photographed by J Frederick Smith, as it appeared in The New Yorker, 17 September 1960. From Ann Marie Brennan's article 'Forecast' in Cold War Hothouses.

Bottom left

'The Bride's House of 1956', House Beautiful, May 1956, back cover. Image from Michael Herman's presentation 'Display' in the seminar 'Cold War HotHouses'.

Bottom middle

Wall of time lines developed in the seminar 'The PhD in Architecture: A Short History', conducted by Beatriz Colomina with the PhD students from Princeton School of Architecture in autumn 2002. It includes: a timeline of the architectural magazines Oppositions, Arquitecturas Bis, L'Architecture d'Aujourd'hui and Casabella, compiled by Joaquim Moreno, mapping the evolution of editorial policies during 1973–4; a time line of student journals from 1950 to the present, including Perspecta, Thresholds, Harvard Design Review, 306090, Via and The Cornell Journal of Architecture, compiled by Ann Marie Brennan, mapping the lineage of contemporary architectural theory; 'Outsiders–Oppositions', a time line by Meredith TenHoor mapping the people, methods and theories 'outside' of architectural culture that influenced the journal Oppositions; two time lines developed by Michael Su mapping the evolution of dissertations in the PhD programme in architecture at Princeton since 1972, in parallel with significant developments at the school.

Bottom right

Postcard announcing the 'Discipline Building: A Short History of the PhD in Architecture' conference at Princeton on 2 and 3 April 2004. Research into this topic was initiated in a PhD seminar run by Beatriz Colomina in autumn 2002.

An article in the recently launched tabloid The Architect's Newspaper measures the success of Bernard Tschumi as the 15-years dean of the School of Architecture, Planning and Preservation at Columbia University in the following terms: 'Its faculty and alumni are constant fixtures in exhibitions, publications and buildings shortlists all over the world.'[1]

Note that not only do exhibitions and publications precede buildings in this listing, but that buildings are not really buildings, but 'buildings shortlists'. That is, whether the buildings get built or not doesn't constitute a measure of success in this account.

Furthermore, whether those architects win the competition or the commission for which they were short-listed seems to be beyond the point as well. It is sufficient if they get short-listed: the project is made, photographed, exhibited, published, critiqued. That is, the project exists as an architectural idea, a form of thought.

Those paying just a little bit of attention would have noticed that in the space of a decade and a half the reception of Tschumi's strategies

at Columbia has gone full circle. From the early years when his efforts to put the school on the map were derided as publicity hype, to full acceptance and praise of these very strategies – this time, however, without any critical assessment of what has really been accomplished.

The same criteria of evaluating architectural success are affecting tenure processes for design positions in schools of architecture all over the US where, for a few years now, the book, the exhibition and the competition entry are the acceptable measures of international recognition for a practising architect.

Paradoxically, this situation brings historians and theorists teaching today in the elite schools of

Discipline Building

architecture in the US closer than they have ever been to so-called practising architects teaching in those same schools, because what these architects are practising is the art of making a book, putting together an exhibition and entering a competition; that is, intellectual activities which involve research, writing, thinking. Meanwhile, the historians and theorists teaching in the same schools are for the most part no longer simply scholars. The majority of us were trained as architects first (for example, Tony Vidler, Stanford Anderson, Michael Hays, Mark Wigley,

Mark Jarzombek, Detlef Mertins, Felicity Scott). Some have continued to practise architecture to some degree (for example, Reinhold Martin, Sarah Whiting, Peggy Deamer, Jennifer Bloomer) and almost all of us are involved in the teaching of design at some level, whether it is actually teaching studio, advising MArch design thesis or acting as design jurors. Even those historians/theorists who were not trained as architects have been involved in studio teaching (for example, Sylvia Lavin, Catherine Ingraham, Bob Somol, Jeffrey Kipnis and Sanford Kwinter). Some of those critics have even become involved in architectural practice. Somol, for example, who has a PhD in the history of culture from the University of Chicago, has recently designed and built a house in LA with his partner, Linda Pollari, to some critical acclaim.[2] Without exaggerating too much, one can say that, today, practising architects in the academy for the most part don't build, while some historians and theorists do.[3]

What are the consequences of this reversal for the teaching of history in our schools?

It may be worthwhile to go back to the 1967 symposium organised by the Journal of the Society of Architectural Historians (JSAH) on 'Architectural History and the Student Architect', a similar event to the one we are taking part in today. Sybil Moholy-Nagy opened the event expressing her dismay over the status of history in schools of architecture with three striking points: 'Why to teach a discipline which is generally rejected by practitioners; whom to select for such an unpopular task; and how to implement the ordeal of four credit units of glazed eyes, chronic absenteeism and interfaculty condescension.'[4]

She rejected the idea that art historians could teach history to architects: 'Repeated experience has shown that they [the art-historical product of our Fine Arts Institutes] are like juvenile alcoholics, in that no matter how sincere their intentions may be of drying themselves out, they will return to the euphoria of Burckhardt, Wolfflin, Panofsky and Greene at the first sniff of a familiar historical interior.' She concluded that only an 'architect of unusual perception and education, or an architectural critic' would be up to the task of teaching history to architectural students.[5]

We cannot claim to be in the same situation today. On the one hand, historians in schools of architecture are largely architects, trained in the PhD programmes inside schools of architecture

that arose as a result of arguments like those of Sybil Moholy-Nagy. On the other hand, far from empty classrooms and glazed eyes, theory and history seminars are oversubscribed at all of the elite schools, and the number and quality of the offerings are often the bone of contention between students and administrators, students being the ones demanding more and better seminars.

We need to reassess the teaching of history in light of the contemporary situation. It is now 30-something years since PhD programmes in the history and theory of architecture began to emerge in universities such as MIT, Cornell, Princeton, Berkeley and Penn. They were preceded by long and elaborate debates on the need for such programmes, both inside the schools and at the universities. Art historians and art-historical methods were found wanting, and the architect-trained historian was seen as a more desirable figure to educate architectural students. PhD programmes were understood as a service to the school of architecture. The service to the service, then, since architecture has always been understood as a service profession.

Much has changed, both on the side of history and on the side of practice. We have ended up with a whole new generation of architectural scholars trained first as designers, but also a whole new generation of practitioners who think of themselves as researchers – because practice has changed too. So much of what goes on in the professional practice of architecture is a form of research. A few years ago this was said only by experimental architects such as Elizabeth Diller and Rem Koolhaas. Today, any architect with a head embraces research and sees his or her work as a specialised form of investigation. It is hard to find an architect who doesn't use the word 'research' as a magic word to describe and legitimise his or her practice. These architects may or may not build, but they definitely are the means by which research is registered in publications, exhibitions, competitions, etc. Competitions are not just ways to get a commission but ways to present innovative research. Publications and exhibitions are not produced to register built work, but to present ways of thinking about architecture.

Yet this remarkable shift did not simply occur over the last 30 years. It's a key part, if not the key part, of the evolution of 20th-century architecture. If, as I have repeatedly argued, the architecture of the last century was produced in the space of photographs, publications, exhibitions, world fairs, magazines, newspapers, museums, art galleries, international competitions, advertising, films, television, computers, and so on – that is, in the space of the media – this obvious fact, almost embarrassing in its simplicity, has been difficult to accept, particularly by academics. It is counterintuitive

to see the history of architecture as a history of ideas rather than a history of buildings; to see that those parts of architectural practice that seem most ephemeral and temporary turn out to have the most permanent effects; to see that a sketch can have more power than any building resulting from it; that three sentences in a magazine can change the course of design; that a pavilion in an international exhibition that nobody saw – 1929 was not exactly a year for tourism – could be proclaimed the most beautiful building of the 20th century.

Paradoxically, practising architects have not had such problems. Alison and Peter Smithson, for example, saw temporary exhibition structures as part of an old tradition going back to the Renaissance and playing a crucial role in stimulating the evolution of ideas and tastes in architecture: 'The architects of the Renaissance established ways of going about things which perhaps we unconsciously follow: for example, between the idea sketchily stated and the commission for the permanent building came the stage-architecture of the court masque; the architectural settings and decorations for the birthday of the prince, for the wedding of a ducal daughter, for the entry of a Pope into a city state; these events were used as opportunities for the realisation of the new style; the new sort of space; the new weight of decoration; made real perhaps for a single day ... the transient enjoyably consumed, creating the taste for the permanent.'[6]

As in the Renaissance, the temporary structures of Modern architecture were staged architecture, a shimmering masque, which

doesn't make the proposal less provocative but perhaps more so. As Peter Smithson put it: 'Like all exhibitions, they live a life of, say, a week or four weeks in reality, then they go on and on forever. Like the Barcelona pavilion before it was reconstructed.'[7]

The temporary turns out to be permanent. Ideas live on. Or, as Andrea Branzi has put it recently: 'Architecture is not simply "something physical" but a much more complex culture, whose projects are forms of thought that interpret the world: I think that the architect of the future should begin with the idea that the energies that transform the city and the territory are not only building activities, but also the powers of imagination and pure research. What has been thought exists.'[8]

Thoughts are reality. What does this mean for the teaching of history in the academy?

A historian should remind the media architect student that the history of architecture is more complex than the history of buildings and building techniques, and that, as Sybil already said in 1967, in the age of the media the 'historical survivors' are the architects who can write, who can reproduce themselves in different media.[9] Reproduction, not understood as the representation of existing work, but with each media treated as a site for the production of new work, new ideas. The greatest architects of the 20th century were all media artists, whose work is embedded within the media campaign they carefully orchestrated. That's why we know them. A question that I like to ask MArch students is how many architects they can name who didn't write. The point is that students have a double interest in history/theory classes: learning about the history of their field and learning how to operate in the present become the same thing. History is indistinguishable from design.

For the PhD students, this blurring of historical

Below
Time line by Michael Su mapping the evolution of the PhD programme in the School of Architecture at Princeton University from 1972 onwards, including information on students, topics, advisers and significant developments at the school. The time line was compiled during the course of the seminar 'The PhD in Architecture: A Short History', conducted by Beatriz Colomina with the PhD students from the School of Architecture at Princeton University in autumn 2002.

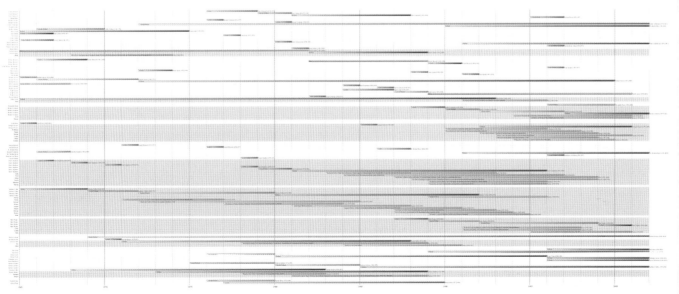

Program in Media and Modernity

Right
Proofs of the cover of the booklet listing classes for the Program in Media and Modernity at Princeton University, autumn 2002. Cover designed by Branden Hookway. The media and modernity programme is an interdisciplinary initiative directed by Beatriz Colomina. It promotes the study of the unique cultural formations that came to prominence during the last century, with special attention on the interplay between culture and technology: the programme centres on architecture, art, film, photography, literature, philosophy, music, history and media from radio to information technology. It offers a graduate certificate and, more broadly, collaborative teaching, learning and research opportunities centred around team-taught seminars and cross-disciplinary colloquia.

Notes
1 Cathy Lang Ho, 'Looking for a leader', The Architect's Newspaper 01, 11/10/2003, p 16.
2 Pollari x Somol House, Los Angeles.
3 I am not talking here about adjunct teaching in the studio, but about full-time academics.
4 Sybil Moholy-Nagy, 'Architectural history and the student architect: a symposium', JSAH 26, October 1967, p 178.
5 Ibid, p 180.
6 Alison and Peter Smithson, 'Staging the possible', in Alison + Peter Smithson, Italian Thoughts (Sweden), 1993, p 16. See also the earlier version of the same argument in 'The masque and the exhibition: stages toward the real', ILA&UD Year Book, Urbino, July 1982.
7 Beatriz Colomina, 'Friends of the future: a conversation with Peter Smithson', October 94, autumn 2000, p 24.
8 Andrea Branzi, 'Modernizing modernity', 109 Provisional Attempts to Address Six Simple and Hard Questions About What Architects Do Today and Where Their Profession Might Go Tomorrow, The Berlage Institute Report, Hunch, 6/7, 2003, p 116.
9 Sybil Moholy-Nagy, 'Since the spread of mass communication, the architect with the greatest verbal capacity has been the historical survivor.' 'Architectural history and the student architect', op cit, p 180.
10 Goethe, quoted by Friedrich Nietzsche in 'On the uses and disadvantages of history for life', Untimely Meditations, trans RJ Hollingdale, Cambridge University Press (Cambridge, MA), 1983, p 59.

research and practice is even more emphatic, since for them research is by definition their practice. If MArch students have to learn that design involves historical production, the PhD students have to learn that history is architectural production.

We have to rethink the way we teach PhD students. Just as doctoral research is informing design in new ways, design could inform doctoral research and pedagogy. The model of the isolated scholar is inadequate. The collaborative applied thinking of design studios can act as a new model for scholarly research. Maybe this is a delayed lesson from Learning from Las Vegas, which pioneered this method in a studio context. One of the most influential theoretical positions emerged out of a studio orchestrated by Denise Scott Brown. In a similar way, the PhD students can work together on a single theme and the results of the research can be made public.

As an experiment, in recent years I have been running a seminar for the PhD students at Princeton where they work in the collaborative spirit of design studios, since architecture is always collaborative, actively carrying out research and presenting it in a book, a conference or an exhibition. The students learn both how to do research and how to put together an event and a publication.

Our first project in the autumn of 2000 was on postwar American architecture. It went for two years of seminars and workshops and has resulted in the book Cold War Hothouses: Inventing Postwar Culture from Plastics to Playboy

(Princeton Architectural Press, 2004). The second project started two years ago with a seminar entitled 'The PhD in Architecture: A Short History', where the intention was to do collaborative research into the unwritten history of PhD programmes. It concluded with a conference in spring 2004 entitled 'Discipline Building'. The resulting book will be different from the first one in that in Cold War Hothouses all of the essays were written by the PhD students participating in the seminar. The second book will mix documentation presented by students (including a number of detailed time lines presenting research in graphic form) and essays by invited scholars.

There is, by now, a large community of scholars and students in the different PhD programmes; generations of writers who are all media architects, like their design colleagues. In preparing conferences, exhibitions and publications, historians in training once again become architects, and are therefore able to directly communicate the lessons of history to designers, allowing history to once again become a vital part of experimental design.

Anyway, these are a few of my thoughts on the future direction of teaching history in schools of architecture. Since I so crudely took the original title of this article from Nietzsche's famous meditation on the uses and disadvantages of history, maybe I should finish with his citation of Goethe at the very beginning of his essay – a citation which captures my feelings as a writer and as a teacher:

'In any case, I hate everything that merely instructs me without augmenting or directly invigorating my activity.'[10] ᐃ

This text was first presented with the title 'On the uses and disadvantages of history for the media architect', at the conference 'Architecture–History–Pedagogy', organised by the History, Theory and Criticism Section of the Department of Architecture, MIT, 21–22 November, 2003.

Peter Lynch

Peter Lynch, architect-in-residence and head of the Graduate Architecture Centre at Cranbrook Academy of Art, provides his overview of architectural education and its changing practice via a tour of the work of Cranbrook students during his tenure at the school.

Architectural Education and Changing Practice

Architectural education has always had a double agenda. It prepares students for the day-to-day practice of architecture and it advances and upholds the culture of architecture – our shared understanding of architecture as a historically defined cultural project, social good and creative endeavour.

So why re-examine architectural education at this moment? There are two answers to this question, corresponding to each of the agendas mentioned above. First, educators must incorporate new technological and social developments within the curriculum in order to prepare students for the changing world of practice. Second, teachers and students seek to understand technological and social changes by asking how they might advance or challenge the broader cultural project of architecture, a search that is hopefully of service to the profession as a whole.

For the past 25 years, Cranbrook's graduate architecture programme has explored changes in architectural practice and culture. Since 1996, during my time as department head, the work has focused on the following questions:

1 What methodologies can reintroduce critical distance – mental space for evaluation and reflection – into the design process? What, besides digital simulation, could replace the orthographic system and other traditional design methodologies?
2 How are the various scales of a work of architecture related? What are the upper and lower limits of form? How can a sense of form extend to smallest scale (the construction unit or element) and largest scale (the region or territory)?
3 How have contemporary architects (and non-architects working in related fields) engaged society in creative and meaningful ways? How can our abilities as architects be brought to bear on real-world problems such as urban disinvestment, suburban sprawl, substandard housing, megapolitan growth, the disappearance of small-town and village life, and destructive settlement patterns?
4 How can the existing 'building delivery system' – the usual approach to design and construction – incorporate greater flexibility and creativity? How can craft be reintroduced into building?

New Methodologies

Before computer-aided design (CAD), orthographic projection was a necessary analytical and representational tool. After CAD

Educators must incorporate new technological and social developments within the curriculum in order to prepare students for the changing world of practice. Teachers and students seek to understand technological and social changes by asking how they might advance or challenge the broader cultural project of architecture.

Opening page
Amy Green Deines, 'Enfold', 2000
'Enfold' is a gangly structure of poplar struts joined by latex 'knuckles' that can form an enclosure within a larger room. The struts can be shaped and reconfigured in much the same way that hair is combed and coifed. Amy Green Deines is one of an increasing number of architecture graduates whose professional practice draws upon industrial design and entrepreneurial business strategies.

Top
Mike Zebrowski, Jeffrey M Rawlins and Bradford Watson, 'Extraction of a Suburban House', 2003
View of demolition process. Over the course of 10 days, the students 'extracted' parts of a worker's bungalow in a Detroit suburb using simple equipment. The chunks were transported by a pick-up truck and trailer to the architecture department, where they were stabilised and slightly modified, then trucked to Tangent Gallery in Detroit. Like many other departmental projects (particularly in the early 1990s under the leadership of Dan Hoffman), this work was strongly inspired by the 1970s site-based sculptures of Robert Smithson and Gordon Matta-Clark.

Middle
'Extraction of a Suburban House', 2003
View of the installation at the Tangent Gallery, Detroit. After the show, some of the house elements were whitewashed and used as permanent administrative facilities for the gallery (reception desk, roll-out exhibition area, offices, etc).

Bottom
Jeffrey M Rawlins, 'Untitled Room (addition)', 2003
This one-room addition is mounted on tracks. It can be docked against the existing worker's cottage and function as additional living space, or be moved into the yard and used as a guest bedroom. The cedar frame, exposed on the interior, is sheathed in Cor-ten steel.

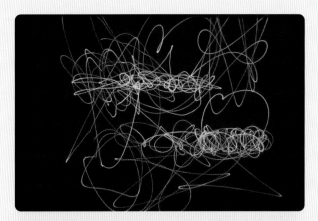

Top
Kenta Kishi, 'Cloud-2: Record of Vibrations', 1997
A time-lapse image of the patterns traced by lights suspended from a crude, slowly rotating gear mechanism. The monotonous, predictable movement of the motor and gears generates complex patterns at this lower level. The project can be understood as an analogy to society – where structures of conformity generate complex outcomes. The effect of a work of architecture could be analogous to the patterns of the pendant lights. The entanglement of the strings supporting the lights creates cloud-like forms, semipredictable and semidefined.

Second from top
Scott Saikley, 'Model of Cathedral', 2002
The project expresses Scott's interest in both Baroque and Gothic architecture. At the same time it is a beautiful example of an 'aggregative' design approach, where simple elements combine in nonperiodic ways to form complex spaces. In this and other examples, the basic element has a 'flaw', or eccentricity, that gives it formal and spatial properties in combination.

Second from bottom
Scott Saikley, 'Plan of Cathedral', 2002
Plan sections at different levels are strikingly different. Radial symmetries and clusters appear at some elevations and disappear at others. As with other schematic projects, tectonic and spatial investigation comes before questions of enclosure and detailing.

Bottom
Kazunori Takeishi, '3456789: A Study in Urban Growth', 2004
Kazu Takeishi is investigating urban sprawl. Rather than denying the architectural significance of this settlement pattern, which would be naive, he is critiquing the status quo and proposing new underlying structures. In the traditional number puzzle the 'magic square', the sequence of ordinal numbers (1,2,3,4...) is placed within a square grid so that the sum in every column, row and major diagonal is the same. If one draws an analogy between the magic square and suburban development, one can posit a settlement pattern that is extremely varied and apparently random, but which has a uniform distribution of functions and infrastructure loads in each direction. To generate the plan, Takeishi superimposed 3x3, 4x4,... to 9x9 magic squares on a one-mile-square site. He represented each number graphically and fractally. Green represents parks and environmental facilities, pink represents high-density consumption, blue represents low-density consumption, yellow represents cultural facilities, and olive, grey and khaki represent housing of different types and densities.

it became a mere convention. All of us trained in the traditional manner understood plan/section/elevation to be a filter or screen interposed between our subjective ideas and their objective realisation. Orthographic projection was a crucible for dissolving private gestures and intuitions and sublimating them into a collaborative work. The indirectness of the orthographic process was not understood to be a disadvantage, although it clearly was an obstacle for anyone who wanted to build precise nonrectilinear spaces. And who knows – perhaps architects like Gaudí or Scharoun saw the difficulty encountered in refining and specifying nonorthogonal elements as something to be respected, to be overcome through virtuosity and ingenuity.

With CAD, the generation and specification of a complex form is no longer an epistemological or intellectual achievement. It is merely a demonstration of technical ability.

Most young architects have abandoned the conceptual framework described above. Different methodologies exist for developing and evaluating ideas. We can easily generate spectacular renderings and animations at early stages of the design process: the perspective image guides the process of design. But as simulation takes the place of representation, the creative process risks becoming more naive. We begin to forget that there is a profound difference between imaginary and inhabited worlds, and that difficulty, labour, destruction and contingency are always involved in the act of building. The very notion of an indirect methodology (like the orthographic system or Alberto Pérez-Gómez's 'perspective hinge') is becoming incomprehensible. Pérez-Gómez and Louise Pelletier are the first to admit that this disappearance has ethical consequences.

'Drawing' may be dying, but it is impossible to revive old methods, no matter how valuable they once were. One cannot base an ethics on nostalgia. What, besides computer simulation and virtual reality, could serve as an effective method for the design process – for the translation of intuitions, desires and needs into physical constructions?

At Cranbrook (and many other places) young architects have a partial answer. Many rely on a way of working that cycles between sketching, computer modelling and the construction of physical models, assemblies and structures, sometimes at full scale. (This is also the method in Steven Holl's office, for example.) Building is a refuge for contemplation and reappraisal. When

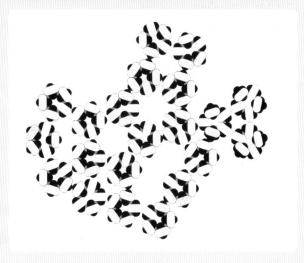

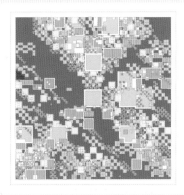

the same 'head and hands' sketches, drafts and
builds, embodied knowledge has space and time
to deepen.

Although it is extremely slow to refine work at
full scale, in some circumstances this slowness
has value: students come to understand the labour
involved in making, and the rhythm and logic of
repetitive, physical and cooperative tasks. In 2003
Jeff Rawlins, Mike Zebrowski and Bradford Watson
dismembered and extracted rooms from a
suburban house, modified them structurally and
installed them as administrative and exhibition
spaces for an art space in Detroit. The
department's large studio spaces allow students
to take on projects that would be inconceivable in
other schools. For example, Jeff prefabricated a
one-room 'house' in the studio and trucked it to his
nearby house, where it was mounted on tracks so
it could dock against the existing structure or sit
independently on the lawn. Many of these students
begin construction without completely planning
their work in drawing form. After that experience
most 'rediscover' the elegance of drawing, not
as a device for fantasy but as an efficient and
integrated step in the construction process.

Scales of Architecture, Limits of Form, Scenarios of Construction

At Cranbrook, students are encouraged to
address the full range of interests that make up
the field of architecture. If we made a diagram
of these scales, it would centre on materials
and sensory phenomena, extending outwards
to the building and finally to the territory.

The middle bands of this concentric model –
including details, assemblies, building, site,
district and urban nucleus – are characterised
by questions of form. ('Form', for me, is a
manifestation of coherence, identity and
boundedness.) Before and beyond this middle
zone the idea of form rarely arises. Materials
and sensations are anterior to questions of form:
one can rarely extrapolate the boundary, image
or organisation of a building from elemental
components, rules or phenomena. Analogously,
at regional or territorial scale, planning and
legislation can rarely define real places or
generate meaningful patterns of settlement and
inhabitation. Urban sprawl is formlessness at
supra-urban scale. Somewhere between the
scale of the element and the scale of the
building, form appears. Somewhere between
the scale of the traditional city and the scale
of the territory, form disappears.

For the past 13 years I have been exploring
the upper and lower limits of form. In my work

I have proposed repetitive, basic construction elements
(bricks, blocks, struts, links and panels) that, when
assembled according to simple rules, compose
structures that are open-ended but which have certain
implicit limits and capabilities. At a larger scale I have
proposed 'open' approaches to planning, where growth
rules and iterative processes of development guide
development towards livable, clearly defined yet not
premeditated urban spaces. (Another goal of this urban
planning and design research is the expression of a
'social form'. If visible form is an expression of physical
boundedness, social form is an expression of collective
boundedness, of a society's autonomy, self-sufficiency
and justice. A metropolitan region that lacks a physical
boundary could yet have a form if its pattern of
settlement expressed an open, characteristic and
harmonious way of life.)

At both upper and lower scales, the goal has been to
invent methods and scenarios of construction that have
a certain elegance, necessity and economy. Many of my
projects for affordable housing, apartment buildings,
institutions, settlements and urban districts have tried
to derive a form 'upwards', from tectonic approaches,
or 'downwards', from urban-planning rules. More
recently my work has tried to directly connect these
smaller- and larger-scale interests.

Students at Cranbrook are attracted to this line
of enquiry. The limit of form is the realm of intuition:
wherever form breaks down, doubt is extremely
productive and rules are open to interpretation.
Students such as Kenta Kishi (1997) used their time
at Cranbrook to construct semifunctional 'analogical
machines' that model the evolution and devolution
of social structures. By extending the analogy into
architecture, Kishi has developed a working method
and a formal language that bridges between
determinism and chance, geometry and chaos.
He is now part of the Tokyo collaborative NIALL.

In the past eight years a number of students have
developed repetitive construction elements that
aggregate or join in nonperiodic ways. The units have
inherent properties, or 'flaws', that limit or direct the
form of the larger-scale structure. Scott Saikley's
2002 pinched-concrete piers, cast in deformed tubes,
are an example of flawed units that define coherent
architectural spaces.

A few students have tackled the larger end of the
scale. Kazunori Takeishi (2004) is modelling urban
sprawl. Using the 'magic square' as an analogy,
he is suggesting new approaches to suburban
development, approaches that could generate extremely
varied spaces and programmatic relationships yet
at the same time allow for a rationally loaded and
balanced infrastructure.

Finally, a few students have proposed methods of
working that make direct connections between the

smallest and largest scales of architecture. In 1999 Greg Vendena made a number of beautiful small-scale urban proposals for Detroit, including cast-iron public seating moulded from discarded chairs. These were gathered together with other small-scale interventions to create informal urban 'constellations', enlivening neighbourhoods on Detroit's east side. (Greg moved to Detroit after graduation and is now realising his projects through the design studio Co-Lab.) This strategy of 'punctuated urbanism' (known from the works of Plecnik, Alvaro Siza Viera and Roberto Collová, among others) has been followed by other students, including Mary Kim in 2002.

Socially and Ethically Grounded Practice

Cranbrook's students are developing more than projects and proposals: each is inventing, for himself or herself, a new and appropriate way to practise. Their interests reflect recent changes in the public and social role of architecture. Some architects, attuned to trends and markets, are increasingly adopting the ahistorical roles of industrial designer or entrepreneur. The work of Amy Green Deines (2000) is a case in point. Architecture, art, fashion, business and design practices now share disciplinary strategies and goals. Architecture is clearly becoming a vehicle for advertising, publicity, fashion, tourism, entertainment and boosterism. At the same time, incongruously, architecture has rediscovered an ethical dimension: consider the growing movements for sustainable design, anti-sprawl urban planning, and refugee, emergency and self-build housing.

For an increasing number of students, a meaningful practice needs to have a conscious social or ethical dimension. Marianne Desmarais is a wonderful example: in 2002, in collaboration with Cranbrook ceramics student Tom Lauerman, she worked with teachers, elementary-school children and other Cranbrook students to establish an educational garden for a Detroit public school. Jeff Sturges, currently a first-year student, is developing, as a business proposition, a convivial tool for communal cooking. These Cranbrook students, and many more like them, are pioneering resourceful, nontraditional approaches to architecture practice. Other Cranbrook graduates who follow the 'straight-and-narrow' professional path, working in their own offices or established firms, are also producing important projects. Each graduate is a reason to be hopeful about the future of architecture. ᴆ

Neil Spiller takes the opportunity to 'smack a few ponies' and express exactly why architectural education, despite its love affair today with new technologies, remains so irrelevant and nostalgic. Spiller's contempt for the reactionary and the anachronistic is counterpoised by the extraordinary images of student work from the infamous Unit 19 at the Bartlett - led by Spiller and his long-time teaching partner Phil Watson.

Neil Spiller

At undergraduate level, students are normally ground down by being taught to conceive of architectural design as a reductive process utilising Victorian construction techniques, sophisticated conceptual thoughts and normative formal vocabularies.

The first important thing for a proper design tutor to do is to inspire the student by opening his or her eyes to what is currently philosophically and technically possible. This often includes reference to the new virtual and biotechnological materials and a quick course in the forgotten, supposedly arcane, thought of others missed or ignored by the mainstream.

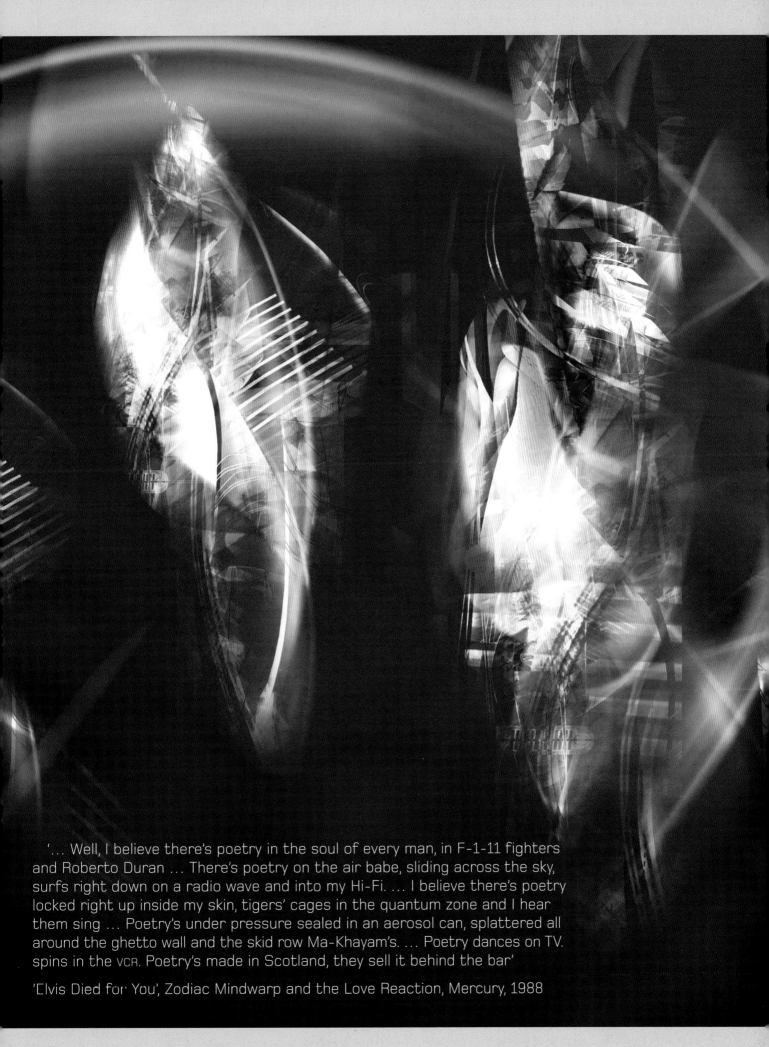

'… Well, I believe there's poetry in the soul of every man, in F-1-11 fighters and Roberto Duran … There's poetry on the air babe, sliding across the sky, surfs right down on a radio wave and into my Hi-Fi. … I believe there's poetry locked right up inside my skin, tigers' cages in the quantum zone and I hear them sing … Poetry's under pressure sealed in an aerosol can, splattered all around the ghetto wall and the skid row Ma-Khayam's. … Poetry dances on TV. spins in the VCR. Poetry's made in Scotland, they sell it behind the bar'

'Elvis Died for You', Zodiac Mindwarp and the Love Reaction, Mercury, 1988

Things We Know

Architectural education is not what it used to be. We know we are part of the planet's infinitely scaled natural ecology. We know that we are on the verge of creating biotechnical architectural devices. We know that a Luddite approach to sustainability will not work. We know that the purely anthropocentric perception of architecture is the blinkered short-sightedness of the architectural donkeys of the last century. We know our cone of vision is no longer conic. We know we can see and sense with a myriad prosthetics, and that because of this our spacescape changes second by second. We know that the great hallowed halls of computing are now small enough to fit into our back pockets. We know we can embroider space in autobiographical wefts (our very own Bayeaux tapestries).

We know that the architectural space purveyed by most architectural schools does not mention any of the above. We know that most of them are complacent and deal in anachronistic, old-world rubbish. We know their reactionary mist is obscuring invention and they are strangling us. We know that architecture, except in exceptional circumstances, has always been the sophist lapdog of commercial imperatives and that this is seldom good. We have read Debord's Spectacle and we see disconnection everywhere. We know that the old guard can't blind our eyes and steal our dreams. We know we will drag the profession into the new millennium, and that the reactionaries (even those masquerading as avant-garde) will have to suck on it.

We know that at the dawn of the 21st century we are capable of making exceptional architectures that immerse themselves in their peculiarities. These conditions can be intensely ecological, systematically open-ended, driven by imperatives of chance, glocal, intellectually founded, enabling, concerned with time and duration, synthetic with natural landscapes, use computational power not just as a means of representation but as an editing spatial engine and, above all, we can create reflexive architecture that can embroider space with swift and changing, exquisite cybernetic chunkings.

These notions give rise to six fundamental paradigms that responsive architecture with any virtual component must deal with:

1 Architects must design in the second aesthetic of the algorithm. This is an aesthetic of programmed possible outcomes or forms and is concerned with the provisions of inputs that are manipulated to produce varying outputs.
2 Architects must choreograph space by manipulating the progression and regression of objects along the virtuality continuum. This continuum ranges from the hard real of 'out here' to full-body inversion in cyberspace 'in there' and the gamut of mixed and augmented realities in between.
3 Natural and machine ecologies form palimpsests of possibilities. The new architecture must respond to the spectacular genius loci of specific sites. Each place is a deep tapestry of space–time vectors.
4 Space and time are not inviolate; they are reversible, collageable and loaded with memory.
5 Biotechnology, nanotechnology and cyberspace have caused the old adages of architecture to collapse: 'Form no longer follows function.'
6 Architectural education can never be the same again. When we educate prospective young architects, we must make them aware of the myriad spaces within and between which architecture can dwell. Spaces whose dimensions unfurl at the click of a digital switch. How do we train the next generation to imagine, use and create sublimity in these obscure jump-cut invigorated spaces? And how will we talk about the aesthetics of this new architecture?

It is my contention that the impact of virtuality and advanced remote-sensing devices should lead architects to reassess Surrealist and pataphysical concepts of space. There are many similarities between these modes of creativity and the way architects might perceive, interact with and make connections between their architecture and the myriad machinic and natural ecologies that constitute the sites of our contemporary architecture.

What I Think

I have been directing the Postgraduate Diploma in Architecture/MArch (Architecture) course at the Bartlett, University College London (UCL) for the last 10 years. I have a hunger for multidisciplinary work. Over this last

Students must understand the political, social and pedagogical dogma to which they have been subjected, and rally against it by positing architectures that question, provoke and make visible the rich world in which we live. They must unchain their brains, and not depend on others for validation.

Students are encouraged to 'site' their work in spatial tapestries (sites) that they can use, reboot, optimise and protect. These interventions must make attempts to respect all of a site's inhabitants (human, animal and vegetal, at all scales).

decade I have been concerned with the dissolution of boundaries between disciplines, advanced electronic technologies and architectural design. For years now I have been encouraging my students away from traditional architectural design towards working in an invigorated spatial spectrum, and to posit objects and ideas that are dynamic and interactive. Because of the ways of traditional architectural education, architects find it hard to think in this way – and it is this way of designing that we will need to master to cope with the accelerated and exponential growth of digital media. Architects can no longer respect the boundaries between disciplines; unbelievable opportunities can be gained from interdisciplinary polycontexturalism. The crossing of these boundaries must first be unfettered by commercial concerns as this leads to the exploration of ideas and concepts that may not solve a particular problem but quite often may shed new light on other problems.

This is not to imply that academe should be insulated from commercial concerns; indeed, many creative opportunities can be found in this domain. In addition, any designer knows that a project is stillborn if it never reaches the building site or the production line. But the load of economic stringency can also weigh down the ideas stage of a project and impair its creative development. Further, student architects need the opportunity to 'turn up all the dials' on their creativity and vision to search for what is possible and not just for what is economically viable at any point in time.

My own research, and that of my students, draws upon a variety of different disciplines to inform architecture. The areas of research are multidisciplinary and include the changing status of the architectural drawing, smart materials, computer-aided architectural drawing, computer-aided manufacture, emergent systems, responsive environments, the architectural design of cyberspace, interactivity, cybernetics, evolving systems and algorithmic design.

Creating responsive, nonprescriptive designs for spatial intervention was the starting point for our interest in the logic of algorithms. These problem–solving diagrams for computer programmers are very useful as a way of describing fluctuating conditions in responsive environments. This led to an interest in other computing paradigms such as cellular automata, complexity and emergence. I have attempted to bring these and other ideas into the arena of architectural design to help student architects

cope with the rapid growth of computational technology that has revolutionised the way buildings are designed, drawn and built.

The new architectures will consist of ecological wefts, technological distortions and, here and there, digital necromancy. The spell is back, mixing together disparate things. Spatial embroidery is where my design is going. It is a world populated by vacillating objects, Dalinian exuberances, and Baroque ecstasies. Architectures will flit across a variety of spatial terrains simultaneously – some seen, some not. Their aesthetic will be conditioned by the 'second aesthetic' of the algorithm – its timings and its nested logics.

The Teetering Condition Within New Architectures
The second aesthetic relies in some sense on the designers' dislocation from their work. This is not new and can be followed back through the work of John Cage, Cedric Price, Gordon Pask and many others. In other words, architects are still mostly unfamiliar with the notion of designing with algorithms to create systems that can create and evolve formal solutions to a variety of inputs. This sort of 'IF/THEN' aesthetic does not have to be used just in a turgid functional way. Rules and conditions can be added that are plainly aesthetic, for example 'If the wind blows in a certain direction then a building occupier's website will have a purple tinge to it for so many minutes'. One might think 'Why would we want to do that?' The answer is because we can now embroider space and objects together across vast distances to achieve a whole new definition of joyful contextuality.

Students are encouraged to design by tweaking the modalities of chance as a way of escaping their own formal fetishisms and creating open-ended architectural systems.

Reading books is vital. Read anything other than architectural monographs. Understand that you make your world, where you are the king of infinite space, or the drunken cyborg named 'clinamen'. They are the same thing really.

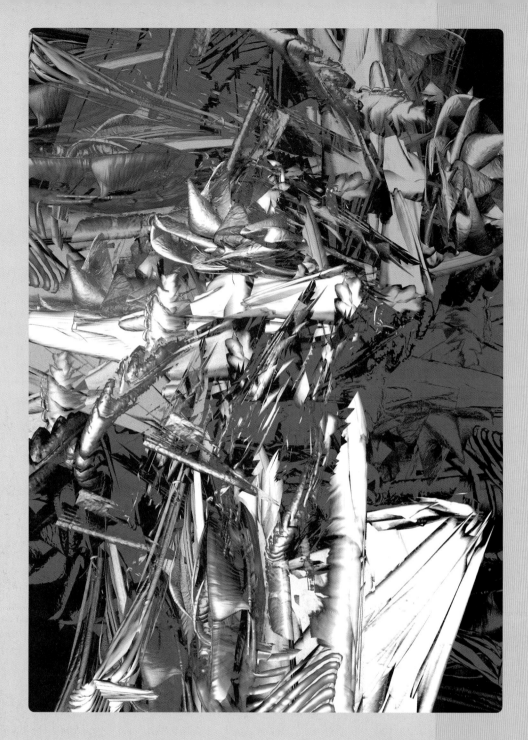

Our profession is a hard one. Its organisation is mostly destructive to really original talent. Students must not feel they are the first, and must know that many have stuck their heads above the parapet before them. These people must be remembered and their ideas understood. They are often excluded from the established canon of architectural history. Students must be aware of the Wilsonian Ninja, have had pizza at the Loaf House, conceive their architecture with an ear to Pask, and dream of the archaeology of the Merzbau to mention just a very few pieces of knowledge crucial to the modern educated student of architecture. Anything less would be criminal.

This notion is where architectural and design education needs to start to attempt to define a new sublime – What is beautiful now? How do these technologies change traditional architectural beauty? In architectural education I speculate that we need to develop processes that are in some way akin to Dali's Paranoiac-Critical Method. This method relies on the flow of psychogeographic and psychosexual associations to liberate Dali from normative thought structures, and would enable us to see and manipulate the huge potentials with which we are presented by the new media. Also, such ideas would help us understand a new aesthetic beauty, in terms of both the 'first' and 'second' aesthetic. This is why Dali, to me, was the last great artist, because he connected high- and low-code objects, developed new object systems of construction, understood the Renaissance magi, had a healthy interest in science, matters spiritual, matters sexual. Some of his notions are very extreme indeed. To appreciate Dali's work, one has to begin to understand an unfamiliar aesthetic and a different aspirational lexicon. We are in a similar condition in respect to information technology today.

The new advanced technologies force space in a myriad of ways, and can collage these together in an ever-shifting 'dance'. Each step of this 'dance' demands a shifting narrative and mythic context that also vacillates. The object changes the spacescape and the spacescape changes the object. The new architectures are forever in search of a million equilibriums that do not exist. This is the 'teetering' condition of contemporary architecture. If we don't make students aware of it, and creative with it, architecture itself teeters into the abyss. △D

Dedicated to Phil Watson, my teaching partner.

Dalibor Vesely

The great stalwart of the University of Cambridge School of Architecture, Dalibor Vesely, explains the philosophy behind postgraduate Diploma studio 1 – an institution in itself.

The first thing that usually comes to mind when we hear about architectural education is its ambiguous nature and uncertain place on the current architectural scene. In conventional understanding, education is seen most often as a separate academic world situated somewhere in the background of the profession. This, rather problematic, vision is not helped by the lack of agreement, between those directly involved in teaching, regarding the role and purpose of education. But the different, and sometimes incompatible, individual positions reflect the general fragmentation of the current architectural scene, and in this sense it is a reality we have to accept as a point of departure.

The phenomenon of fragmentation and fragment became an important part of my thinking a long time ago. My first years in practice, and even more so my first competitions, very quickly brought home the contrast between the cooperative atmosphere of the studio and the polarisation of the professional world. This became even clearer when I had the opportunity to sit on several competition juries. What I found problematic was not the difference of position and opinion, but their incompatibility.

And yet, the incompatibility of individual positions is not something given, but rather a result of the one-sided cultivation of differences in what we share. Today, architects seem to be more aware of the differences that separate them and give to their work an aura of novelty and originality. This leaves behind the common references and goals that contribute to the long-term cultural relevance of their work. The emphasis on difference and originality leads not only to the merit of the results being questionable, but also to an isolation from the world which we all, in one way or another, share.

In the culture I come from, this problematic relation to the shared world was already a major issue for the prewar avant-gardes. Strong Romantic individualism was challenged by an equally strong need for unity, as is evident in the manifesto of the international progressive artists (who included Dadaists, Futurists, Surrealists, International Modern architects, and so on): 'From all over the world come voices calling for a union of progressive artists. Art needs the unification of those who create. Art must become international or it will perish.'[1] It is rather symptomatic that most such attempts failed, owing to a dilemma between the need for participation and a much stronger desire for individual freedom and emancipation. This seemed to confirm a historical inevitability of fragmentation.

Nevertheless, at the same time the nature of fragmentation (and fragment) was viewed differently within some avant-garde movements, particularly in Cubism and Surrealism, where fragment played a new, restorative role in relation to the given reality. A similar tendency can be found on a philosophical level in the phenomenological movement and its discovery of the primacy of the life world. Here, the restorative role of fragment was closely associated with its metaphorical nature, pointing to the implied wholeness of reality to which the fragment actually, or potentially, belongs. Cubist painting illustrates very well the transformation of the negative role of fragment, leading to fragmentation, into a vehicle of poetic enhancement and synthesis. The transformation depends on fragments encountering each other, which reveals through their similarity and analogy a common level of shared reality.

In painting 'the subject', Braque explains: 'For instance a lemon next to an orange, ceases to be a lemon and an orange – they become fruit.'[2] There is a close analogy between the role of fragment in painting and in architecture, where it can represent many different things – the explicit elements of space such as furniture, walls, windows, staircases, structural systems, and so on, but also abstract programmes and briefs, as well as relatively isolated areas of broader culture available as potential reference. Taken together the individual elements can be treated either as a system or as a genuine communicative space. The first option does not usually lead to a satisfactory architectural solution, because as the Romantics were already aware: 'Even the largest system is after all only a fragment.'[3] The second option depends on our ability to establish meaningful (mostly metaphorical) links between the individual elements of space, which reveal their deeper common ground, the foundation for the creation of the true (genuine) communicative space.

It is encouraging to see that behind the

silence of mutually isolated negative fragments there is a potential world of communication which can be, under certain conditions, recovered and articulated. The role of architecture and visual arts in the restoration of the communicative space illustrates how it is possible to overcome the current state of fragmentation; not only in the sphere of arts but in culture as a whole.

This is obviously only a brief description of the framework in which the main task of current architectural education should be, as I see it, situated. The key place for all educational activities is the studio. I believe very strongly that any exploration, investigation or research into the programme and content of a project should be based on a visual hypothesis of the project and focused on what I would describe as a 'situational' approach, in which the spatiality of typical situations is the primary vehicle of design. Situations represent the most complete way of understanding the condition of our experience of the surrounding world and the human qualities of the world. They also endow experience with durability, in relation to which other experiences can acquire meaning.[4] Structural, material or any other more specific consideration should be preceded by a free imaginative exploration of the possible spatial configurations, following the criteria of the situational experience and meaning based on the content of the project.

In most of our projects, content is seen in a nondogmatic way, and rather broadly. As a result we have learned much about typical situations, such as reading, listening to music, working, dining, and so on, from painting, theatre, film, literature and other more distant areas of culture. In the interpretation of the different contributions, we are using metaphorical visual studies, similar in their nature to the nature of a clearly structured collage. Metaphorical studies proved to be a very useful medium to open the horizon of reference into areas of culture and experience that would otherwise be difficult to translate into architecturally relevant results.

This brings us to what I would describe broadly as 'literacy'.

How much do we need to be informed, and what and how much should we know as architects or designers? Current education is mainly oriented towards technical subjects, and yet most of these subjects are already firmly in the hands of engineers who are usually better qualified and equipped for the task. There is no doubt that architects should be at home in that

Above right
Diploma studio 1, civic zone of the Spitalfields project, 1987
This shows the location of the facilities capable of reconciling commercial and civic interests, examples of which include: the centre for experimental and electronic music (diagonal building in the garden); research laboratories (glass tower); and the shadow theatre (curved space). The remaining part of the central space (garden) is left free for future development.

Right
Adam Robarts, composite representation of the shadow theatre, the Spitalfields project, 1988
The theatre is developed on two levels, the first addressing the primary conditions of the performance space, such as the visibility of events, material texture of space and the role of light, the second addressing the metric configuration of space. The tension between these two levels represents a creative dialogue leading to the final stage of design.

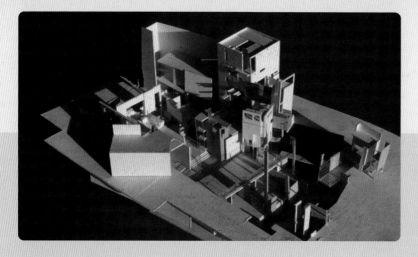

Above
Adam Richards, International Centre of Comparative Literature, St Peter's district, Prague, 1992
The project explores the relation between the complexity of the programme and the most appropriate spatial arrangement, investigating the merit of spatial integration (lecture and seminar rooms, dining, exhibitions, and so on) and relative autonomy of spaces and rooms (library, reading, private studies, etc).

Right
Adela Askandar, Vienna media centre and library, 1999
View of the electronic library and reading room. The composite technique, based on the computer representation of the primary spatial structure, is used here to explore the possibilities of a nonperspectival, fully developed situational arrangement of working spaces. The final character of the space is defined by transparent links between individual areas and places.

Notes
1 'Founding proclamation of the Union of Progressive International Artists', in S Bann (ed), The Documents of Twentieth Century Art: The Tradition of Constructivism, Thames & Hudson (London), 1974, p 59.
2 B Zurcher, Georges Braque: Life and Work, Rizzoli (New York), 1988, p 155.
3 F Schlegel, 'Aus den Heften zur Poesie und Literatur', in F Schoningh, Kritische Schriften und Fragmente, Verlag (Paderborn), 1988 (fr 930).
4 For a more detailed discussion see my Architecture in the Age of Divided Representation, MIT Press (Cambridge, MA), 2004, pp 346–52.

significance for me – how it contributed to the literacy and the visible quality of design. The emphasis on literacy has much to do with my own early education, which was strongly influenced, on the level of thinking, by the tradition of phenomenology, and, on the level of visual skills and culture, by the unique combination of the Constructivist tendencies and Surrealism.

The question of literacy can be treated in the studio as a visual representation of typical situations (library, museum, dwelling, city street, and so on) based on the study of the same, or similar, examples from the past (historical precedents) but also on the representations of such examples in painting, theatre, literature, or in any other area of culture that appears relevant. The extension of the narrowly (mostly technically) defined design tasks into a broader context of culture can be achieved by the cultivation of situational thinking, which takes into account the presence of latent architecture at least in painting and literature. It is in these areas that the richness of human situations is most explicitly articulated and can help us to understand what is essential in each concrete case.

What has interested me in recent years is the problem of representation in relation to the distance that separates the possibilities of visual and conceptual representations (simulations, virtual reality) and the reality of the phenomenal world. We have explored the problem of representation in several projects in the studio, using as a vehicle the structure of typical (paradigmatic) situations, which helped us to restore some continuity between the conceptual and phenomenal levels of design, for example between imaginary, digitally generated spatial structures and the corporeal (material) nature of space.

Perhaps the most important role of the typical situations we have explored is their capacity to situate different individual positions and contributions to the broader scene of design in a framework we can share and use to reduce the current level of cultural fragmentation. This is particularly relevant in addressing the problems of the city, which are, even today, a result of multiple contributions and not of a single plan or a vision of a genius. In our projects, situated mainly for these reasons in the urban setting, we have explored different possibilities to overcome the limits of individual knowledge and vision by dividing larger problems into segments (treated as individual projects), and then negotiating their plausible integration. The diversity and unpredictability of the process brings the results closer to the concrete reality of the situations addressed in the projects, and by implication to the more authentic reality of the city. The attempt to restore the dimensions of solidarity and cooperation in design is based on the belief that culture depends not so much on what we have or can do individually, but on what we can share. ∆

field, but they don't have to emulate the work of the engineers or claim to be technical experts. On the other hand, there are issues and areas of knowledge specific to architecture, such as the experiential, social and cultural role and meaning of space, which are seriously under-represented in most school curricula. And yet this is an area of experience and knowledge that represents the primary conditions of any successful design. Architectural education should face more seriously the choice between the cultivation of knowledge and expertise specific to architecture, and the pessimistic alternative that most of the architectural questions will be answered in the form of applied engineering.

Returning to the work in the studio, it became clear to me quite early that architecture must be defended on more than one level, including the level of knowledge which should be supported by knowledge from the sphere of humanities, so far the weakest part of our education. This brought me, to some extent against my will and quite early in my career, to the study of history, philosophy and humanities.

However, this extended area of knowledge had, in the end, always only one primary

Brett
Steele

As the cofounder of D[R]L, the Design
Research Lab, at the Architectural
Association in London, **Brett Steele**
has launched an entirely new kind
of postgraduate curriculum. Steele
describes how D[R]L has striven to
create a programme that embraces
current multidisciplinary, while also
promoting self-organised teamwork
and integrated research.

Above left
Brett Steele with the thesis studio teams, D[R]L John Street studios, November 2002
The D[R]L is a 16-month post-professional course in architectural design, leading to a Masters of Architecture (MArch) degree. Our studio-based course develops advanced skills and knowledge through the making of detailed design proposals for new, alternative forms of architectural and urban space. The D[R]L treats design projects as a form of shared research, and emphasises a rigorous, analytical and thoroughly documented investigation into all design results and parameters shaping a project. Studio, workshop and seminar courses focus on the challenges of new and emergent spatial formations, including their social organisations, technologies and design implications.

Above right
D[R]L Phase II thesis studio team '+RAMTV' presenting their final project, Architectural Association Lecture Hall, January 2002
Innovation As Collaboration: The Open-Source Studio. All design and research projects are pursued as collective proposals and are undertaken in small, self-organised teams addressing common topics through shared information-based diagrams, data, models and scripts. The D[R]L studio at John Street is the centre for its team-based approach to teaching and learning. Each year the D[R]L establishes a year-long design agenda which is then used to coordinate the design of its individual studio, workshop and seminar courses, integrating and focusing the most productive results of the previous year's work. The D[R]L's internal LAN and wireless networks connect all current participants and design teams, and are treated as a vital design system in the studio. These networks link teams' shared applications, programming experiments, project files and design results in real time, while also providing a continuously updated, elastic archive of all past and present D[R]L work. Upon arrival, all new students gain immediate access to this key learning resource.

1 Distributed Design Systems

> 'It's better to be good, than to be original.'
> — Mies van der Rohe

Consider my remarks here a kind of machinic manifesto – an automated call not written by me so much as automatically forwarded to you via this issue of Δ, and composed by my open-source word processor.[1] The subject of this message is an appeal for new team-based and research-oriented forms of architectural education, needed today in the face of new ways of working, their design technologies and the expanded scope of architectural invention.

It's time for what the philosopher of science Thomas Kuhn[2] once called a paradigm shift; a dramatic change in the conceptual framework through which design innovation is pursued. Schools must move away from an emphasis on 'personal creativity' (idiosyncratic, proprietary forms of architectural knowledge) and towards more rigorous forms of collective understanding and experimentation. I've discussed the realities of today's distributed, machinic design tools elsewhere; I'm interested here in their educational implications and the ways in which they create a need for new forms of shared, open-source design collaboration.[3]

Peer-to-peer learning is fast becoming a routine feature of our working lives. An online search I did late last night at a favourite MEL/Maya site (looking for a snippet of code to refine an IK model I'm working on) showed that some of the projects recently uploaded there had already been downloaded by several thousand users.[4] Today's designers are constantly swapping the files, scripts, images and plug-ins that are essential parts of their work.

A generation ago, Marshall McLuhan noted that the modern classroom seating plan 'persists in the spatial layout of the movable types which gave us the printed page'.[5] Today's new information technologies make some spaces like these feel like classical forms of architecture.

Learning and and exchange outside of schools and academies have been a crucial (and remarkably undertheorised) part of Modern architecture. Recall that pioneers like Mies,

Corb or Wright didn't even attend architectural schools, and remember, too, the indelible impact of Modern architectural media in transferring architectural knowledge person-to-person beyond traditional educational settings (the 1911 European publication of the Wasmuth Portfolio created virtual clones of Wright in such faraway places as the Netherlands).[6] Today's peer-to-peer networking technologies[7] spectacularly accelerate these kinds of experiences, and schools must reorganise their internal teaching strategies to more effectively emulate the smooth forms of exchange that are at the heart of new media.[8] My belief in this is based upon my experience first designing, and now directing, the D[R]L.

2 The D[R]L

> 'The classroom is now a place of detention, not attention. Attention is elsewhere.'
> — Marshall McLuhan

Seven years ago we created the Design Research Lab (D[R]L) at the Architectural Association (AA) as a new kind of graduate design programme. The D[R]L treats today's network-based design systems not as topics to think about, but rather as the basis for an entirely new kind of design curriculum; one that promotes self-organised teams rather than isolated individual students. In creating it we looked for inspiration at a deliberately wide variety of sources; at such diverse phenomena as Napster (or later Kazaa); at the unrealised post-structural pedagogy of Gregory Ullmer's 'applied grammatology';[9] at the open-source genius of Linux; and at the modern group architectures of previous generations (shared work embodied in CIAM, Team X and others). We examined the history of multitasking, management theories, cross-disciplinary artists and today's new economy business plans. We even worked with corporate innovators like Microsoft UK, Ove Arup, M&C Saatchi and Razorfish, examining in detail how they structure their own creative work and how they use their existing office spaces.[10]

The curricular structure we created for the D[R]L differs from how most design schools are organised in two important ways. Firstly, our students undertake only a single long-term design research project during their time with us (rather than a series of short and unrelated design exercises).[11] The project unfolds over

Above
D[R]L studio workshop teams working simultaneously on documents shared across studio networks, D[R]L Tottenham Court Road studios, spring 2001
Networks As Design Tools: Distributed Design Systems. Small design teams act as independent nodes within the studio's networks, directing the development and flow of projects through software modelling applications, programming languages, scripting protocols and other digital design and production systems. The D[R]L seeks to explore the potentials being created within this distributed electronic realm of design disciplines, treating these new design systems as an active, synthetic material in which modern innovations of space are being surpassed today by an even more modern proliferation of interface. Far from heralding an end to architecture's traditional professional roles, the explosion of new design interfaces suggests a need for a new generation of designers able to negotiate these complex networks. This new generation is being shaped, above all, by the demands of their shared, standardised design systems and the protocols of their associated artificial programming languages. The D[R]L focuses on the new forms of design thinking and skills needed to capture, control and shape an endless flow of information across these rapidly evolving systems, which now link designers, clients, users and operating systems in fundamentally new and unexpected ways.

Notes
1 OpenOffice v.1.1.0 is a free multi-platform office productivity application that works with all Microsoft® file formats. OpenOffice.org source code includes technology by Sun Microsystems and is written in C++ to deliver language-neutral and scriptable functionality, including Java APIs. The technology introduces next-stage software architecture, including XML-based file formats. It is available at www.openoffice.org/product/index.html This essay was written, researched, copied and printed without proprietary software of any kind.
2 Thomas S Kuhn, The Structure of Scientific Revolutions, 3rd edn, University of Chicago Press (Chicago), 1996, p 10.
3 For a discussion of these systems, see Brett Steele, 'Disappearance and distribution: the architect as machinic interface', in Hunch 6/7, ed Jennifer Sigler, Berlage Institute (Amsterdam), 2003, pp 422–36.
4 www.highend3d.com/maya/ provides a good example of these kinds of online resources. Links also provide extensive tutorials, manuals and other guides, including discussion groups and ways of connecting the Maya modelling environment to other applications, interfaces and systems.
5 In Eric McLuhan and Frank Zing (eds), Essential McLuhan, Independent Pub Group, 1995, p 285.
6 Within a decade of FLW's Wasmuth

16 months, allowing knowledge and skills to emerge gradually into comprehensive and detailed final results. The second important ingredient is a more radical difference from conventional architectural teaching: our students only ever work in small self-organised teams – of students, but also and, just as importantly, of collaborators, consultants and tutors.

An important additional aspect is that all work is done across high-speed LAN and, now, wireless networks that connect the teams to servers that make all project data available to everyone else as part of an open-source, non-proprietary, approach to design. These servers now contain project files (in usable modelling formats and code) dating right back to our first generation of students in 1997. Setups like this are becoming an essential design tool in their own right, and are evolving into valuable extensions of design teams.

Augmented design networks such as this are an essential aspect of our pedagogy in the D[R]L, which can be thought of as a programme in the dual sense – an academic one as well as a piece of software (in the language of programming, an operating system merging the realms of curriculum and software into a single seamless diagram).[12]

But this assimilation of network technologies is only one of many new features describing the conditions of today's globalised design disciplines. Instead of treating them as a theme or topic for critical reflection,[13] we've openly embodied the processes associated with globalisation as the basis for other changes in how we think design should now be taught. This includes, for example, the actual make-up of an intelligent learning environment today: we began this academic year with 80 students in the D[R]L, who joined us from more than 30 different home countries. It's a kind of rampant internationalisation that represents another signal feature of today's globalised design disciplines.

As one indication of our distributive instability, not one of our first 200 graduates – or staff – began their education in the UK. Our students have been initially educated in Chile, Poland, Taiwan, New Zealand, Canada, Bahrain, France and the US. They speak Mandarin, Russian, Hindi, Greek and

An extreme collaborative mix creates the conditions, I believe, for a genuinely new and distributed kind of architectural intelligence. With it, a more openly research-based approach to architectural knowledge is possible.

countless other native languages, although (interestingly) more now arrive already able to easily communicate with their classmates through artificial programming languages (like AutoLisp, MaxScript or Visual Basic) than any of their home languages. This kind of extreme collaborative mix creates the conditions, I believe, for a genuinely new and distributed kind of architectural intelligence. With it, a more openly research-based approach to architectural knowledge is possible.

3. Design as Research

'An education revolution ... requires the reversal of our present system of compartmentalization of knowledge and of going from the particular to the even more special.'
— Buckminster Fuller

Large-scale research and development (R&D) enterprise is a universal trait of advanced economies, industries and policy. Every year industry and market leaders, intent on keeping their market positions, invest billions of dollars in an effort to uncover new products, technologies and ideas (even as secure a company as Microsoft now spends in excess of $1 billion a year researching new ideas). This dedication to research has long been the rule in science and industry, and is increasingly a feature of other areas of life.[14]

Decades ago, American universities (some employing hundreds, or even thousands, of researchers within a single institute) dramatically changed how academic sciences were pursued, and in so doing also created entirely new standards for the open exchange of knowledge and information across local groups of

Frank Gehry's office, for example, has spent years transferring technologies from the aerospace industry into architectural applications now used by the firm. At Foster and Partners a similar kind of office-wide research and development group has been formed, and at Arup several independent teams offer expert support to their offices world-wide.

specialists and interested professionals; an increasingly common feature of contemporary architectural practice.[15] A dedicated research and development group at Frank Gehry's office, for example, has spent years transferring technologies from the aerospace industry into architectural applications now used by the firm. At Foster & Partners, a similar kind of office-wide research and development group has been formed, and at Arup several independent teams offer expert support to their offices world-wide (including their Advanced Geometries Group and an Arup Research and Development department). In another vein, Rotterdam-based OMA has established its own sister firm (called AMO) whose work is dedicated to research distinct from any of the firm's high-profile building projects.

Research has played a key role within the history of Modern architecture; recall modern pioneers like Prouvé (who developed hybrid architectural forms out of close work with the

French aeronautical industries), the Eames (their Moulded Plywood Division) or Buckminster Fuller (whose individual projects are case studies for many research interests).

Experimental forms of design research are also a growing part of contemporary education, seen in 2000 on prominent display in Greg Lynn and Hani Rashid's 'Architectural Laboratories', which was created with their students at the Venice Biennale.[16] This interest in experimental research has, as well, been important in modern architectural education, which emerged in settings such as the Bauhaus, where teaching focused not on 'architectural' topics but rather on new industrial processes, media and manufacturing (somewhat remarkably, there wasn't a single architecture course taught at the Bauhaus during its first eight years).[17]

This advance grew out of Henry van de Velde's original Weimar curriculum, which insisted that student designs be reached only through a rigorous analysis of a project's problems rather than the application of a preconceived design formula. The belief was later codified in the 1930s and 1940s at schools like Mies's IIT in Chicago or Gropius' ETH, or in the 1950s the Höchschule für Gestaltung in Ulm. A decade later, research-driven pedagogies sprung up at places like Frei Otto's Institute for Lightweight Structures in Stuttgart, and in the 1970s a host of educational experiments flourished. These included the hailed (and much-copied) 'unit system' installed by Alvin Boyarsky at the AA, which replaced a developmental approach to learning with intensely focused (year-long) forms of design research.

Other experimental work was undertaken at the time at SCI-ARCH in Los Angeles (a school created when its

Folio, an architect like Dudok appears in the Netherlands and turns his hometown of Hilversum into a kind of European Oak Park. See Maristella Casciato, 'The Dutch reception of Frank Lloyd Wright: an overview', in Martha Pollak (ed),The Education of the Architect: Historiography, Urbanism, and the Growth of Architectural Knowledge, MIT Press (Cambridge, MA), 1997, pp 139–57.

7 For a discussion of these new technologies, see Andy Oram, Peer-to-Peer: Harnessing the Power of Disruptive Technologies, O'Reilly (Sebastopol), 2001.

8 A widely admired model of online collaborative (that is, distributed and self-organising) filtering of technical knowledge can be found at www.slashdot.org. For a discussion of the contemporary notion of collaborative filtering, see Steven Johnson, Emergence: The Connected Lives of Ants, Brains, Cities and Software, Allen Lane (London), 2001, pp 161–2.

9 Gregory Ullmer, Applied Grammatology (E-Pedagogy from Jacques Derrida to Joseph Bueys), The Johns Hopkins University Press (Baltimore, MD), 1985.

10 These and other companies have served as quasi-clients for our teams' research and design projects, and have allowed generous access for our teams' extended research into how they work in their existing office spaces.

11 Our complete manual for the program, available in html and .pdf formats, can be found at www.aaschool.ac.uk/aadrl/html/pros pectus0304/html/aadrlCourseguide_index.html.

12 D[R]L v. 7.1 is our seventh intake of new students participating in this experiment. The program was beta tested in our first year, 1996/97, and the current release 7.1 was launched in October 2003 at the beginning of the academic year. Like any piece of software, we continue to tweak the program constantly, based on user feedback, new technologies and annual adjustments in design agendas.

13 For an example of a recent negative dialectics that awkwardly equates globalised design with globally available design 'products' (what amounts to a [post-] post-structuralism of consumer critical theory), see Hal Foster, Design and Crime (And Other Diatribes), Verso (London), 2003.

14 For a compelling history of the unexpected ways in which large-scale research and development projects lead to design innovation, see WE Bijker, TP Hughes and T Pinch (eds), The Social Construction of Technological Systems, MIT Press (Cambridge, MA), 1987.

15 Peter Galison and Caroline A Jones, 'Trajectories of production laboratories/factories/studios', in Hans Ulrich Olbrist and Barbara Landour Linden (eds), Laboritorium (Antwerp), 2001, pp 205–10.

16 Greg Lynn and Hani Rashid, Architectural Laboratories, Netherlands Architecture Institute (Rotterdam), 2002.

17 See Marty Bax, Bauhaus Lecture Notes 1930 1933, IDC Publishers (Amsterdam), 1991, p 45. During the school's first eight years the only directly architectural experience available to Bauhaus students was working in Gropius's office. Following student protests in 1926, Hannes Meyer added the first architectural course to the school's curriculum in 1927.

18 Rem Koolhaas, Conversations with Students, Princeton University Press (Princeton, NJ),1996, p 59.

19 One ex-graduate from the Kahn years at Penn once told me that the school received nearly 1,200 applications during the year that he applied in the late 1960s – for a total of less than two dozen places offered by the department that year.

20 For a discussion of multiplicitous, nearly schizophrenic forms of subjectivity today, see Deleuze and Guattari, A Thousand Plateaus: Capitalism and Schizophrenia, Continuum (London), 1991.

teachers fled more traditional universities); at John Heyduk's Cooper Union in New York; and Daniel Libeskind's Cranbrook Academy in Detroit, all of which developed highly personal, nonetheless incredibly rigorous and systematic forms of experimentation); or Peter Eisenman's IAUS Institute in Manhattan. In traditional university settings, educators such as Robert Venturi or Colin Rowe literally fled the traditional space of the design studio in the 1960s and 1970s in pursuit of design research, taking students on extended projects that became the material for Learning from Las Vegas and Collage City (Koolhaass' contemporary Harvard Project on the City emulates this migratory path).

However, these innovative experimental efforts were, and remain, the exception to the uniform standards of professional architectural education; a beige backdrop upon which a fictive image of the architect as a combative 'creative individual' has continued to flourish. (As Koolhaas has written: 'Academies have contributed to dismantle architecture's ambitions, rather than to exercise them.').[18]

Architecture schools worldwide still cling to an almost obsessive belief in promoting individual designer creativity and autonomy. This modern equation of personality and pedagogy reached some kind of high-Modern zenith in the bizarre 1960s fame of Louis Kahn, who briefly attained such cult-like status during his years teaching at Penn that gaining admission to the school became a virtual lottery.[19] Kahn's entire pedagogy (the design techniques of which

included such idiosyncrasies as smudged charcoal and an ability to hold conversations with masonry) disappeared from architecture discourses about as quickly as did Kahn following his sudden death in 1974.

An educational affirmation of architectural 'individuality' neatly mirrors the profession's modern fascination with signature styles, consolidated as the basis for their one-on-one learning methods. This therapeutic model of learning (associated with an imagined 'experience' gained by confrontation/confession between student and teacher) has become the worst kind of machinic diagram – one whose principal output is arbitrary designer differentiation. Today's studio-based teaching methods have become a kind of grotesque parody of Modernism's desire for singular, monolithic forms of subjectivity – an increasingly troubled concept many now seek to dismantle – in order to see students, teachers, design tools and, especially, any concept of a designer's 'identity' as inherently unstable and multiplicitous.[20] To do so is to anticipate a wholly new kind of learning environment.

Architecture schools are still relatively young in historical terms. Their survival (let alone appearance) shouldn't be treated as a historical inevitability. Professional design schools were originally the product of European intellectual enterprises that began in the 17th and 18th centuries, were greatly systematised in the academies of the 19th century, modernised and, then, largely industrialised at the beginning of the 20th. Since then they have settled into increasingly stable, inert forms. Their survival during the 21st century will depend on their willingness to adapt to the multiple forces already reshaping how architects now live, work and learn. ∆

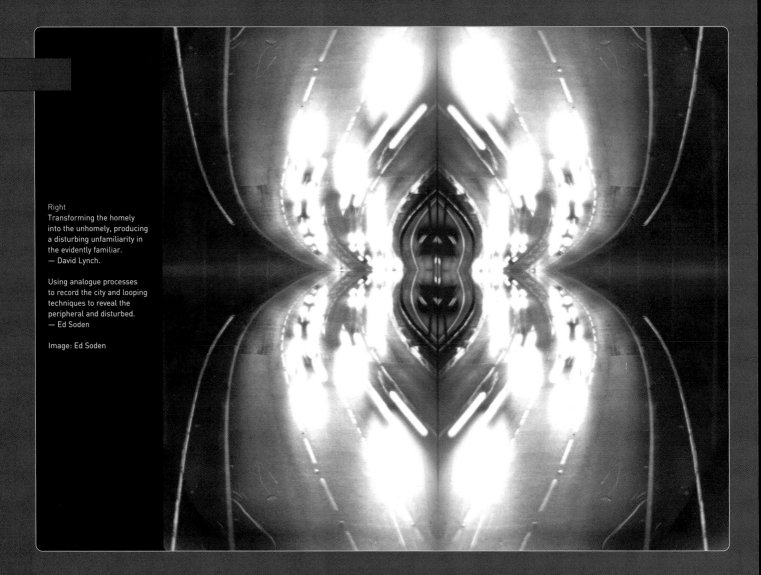

Michael Chadwick

Michael Chadwick discusses his perceptions of education as a young tutor teaching across architecture schools in London. What role must education take in the future and how might it be possible to resolve the contradictions between education and practice? Featured parallel texts and images are by former students: Ana Rute Faisca, Jenny Moore, Ed Soden and Eva-Chloe Vazaka.

The following are some thoughts on the Kafkaesque condition experienced in the dualism of the institution of architecture through the two fields of education and practice, outlined through the use of some key words, conditions and texts.

The initial experience of the uncanny is usually contained and defined within various other topics, but more recently is becoming evident in the contradiction of architecture in the relationship between education and practice. The definition of the sensation of 'uncanniness' is generally difficult to explain. However, in architectural education it is the confusion of subjective/objective and reality/surreality that provides this contradiction and uncanniness, mutating the subject into a replication of itself in the 'otherness' of a schitzophrenic parallel world. This is a world devoid of architecture's realities due to the psychological split caused by the institutionalised personalities of education and practice, each of whom is fighting for domination over the other.

This is most apparent in the design project thesis in which the uncanny feeling is strongly linked to a form of intellectual uncertainty, to the philosophy of what the thesis is grounded upon in the subject of architecture. It materialises through the transformation of a perceived

EDUCATIONAL REALITY

'Experiments often test the experimenter more than the subject. One remembers the old joke about the laboratory rat who said "I have that scientist trained – every time I press this lever he gives me a pellet of food".'
The University of Death : The Atrocity Exhibition'J G Ballard

PULLING TOGETHER

Part of the education of an Architect is to bring everything together for the final presentation. All of a sudden we have to make all connect with some sort of twisted turn of fate. All this time I have failed to find a reason for combining and summarising but then again I haven't really asked anyone either. In the process "of pulling together" apparently everything needs to start at the beginning and finish at the end regardless whether the process followed by each student. I have worked illogically and now I have to squeeze it into logic. And to top it up we have to fit everything onto two panels.

In this process we all feel the pressure of finding a very clever way of "pulling together" because suddenly we became aware that all our work could be lost.
I now strongly believe that architectural education is like a soap opera. If we quickly bring to mind any soap all the characters involved are strictly within a framework, which pre-exists to the script and the actors. Nothing changes; there is no escape from the boundaries of presenting a non-real view of life. I have often wondered how tutors are not bored doing the same thing every year. If by miracle the opportunity arises they make sure that it will not surface.

The presentation becomes more important than the project, so anyone can lie and graphically trick the viewers. And you can not imagine how willing tutors are to be lied to.
So final presentations are not about an outcome but about advertising. There is a valuable lesson.

13
05
03

Above
Educating An Architect
The paradox of (educating) an architect is demonstrated in every event of (student) life. Under pressure of invading a tranquil landscape of a slowly disintegrating site, I felt compelled by the idea of a school of architecture being the entire world, being everyday life – thoughts, perceptions and experiences. Could this possibly be simply interpreted into an enclosure? Even if it could, why should it? The brief altered holistically. It no longer acquired the physical form represented as a potential material world through the conventionality imposed on every evolved concept of non-materiality. Through an entropic process of recording, examining and challenging, the project became an education itself, by illustrating, in parallel, life and expectations.

Image and text: Eva-Chloe Vazaka

Below
The sense of unease is partly a product of cross-generic confusion, perceived by the absence of those rules and conventions that afford comfort, and most importantly orientation.
— Anthony Vidler.

Mining footage and recomposing the ready-made creates a world where head-on collisions occur and trains disappear.
— Ed Soden

Image: Ed Soden

---

homeliness of the architectural processes of creation and analysis, the aspects of the unhomely causing a disturbing unfamiliarity in that which was originally familiar. This is manifested in the contradiction of the representation of architecture generally, and the use of practice criteria as a tool for analysing the creative processes within education.

In fact, in producing the mutation of 'otherness', the field of practice is virally attempting to attain symbiosis with education. Typically, the ideal situation for a virus is to replicate within its host without in any way disturbing the host's normal metabolism, creating a total symbiosis of wholly benign equilibrium. Unfortunately, practice is devouring education with its virus, causing a biological mutation that occasions alterations in those aspects of the host that survive. This causes any equilibrium of the symbiotic relationship to break down and progress to actual and full assimilation of education by practice, whereby the definitions of each will become undefinable.

To remedy this we must look at education and practice individually, and how each functions separately. But first we need to disentangle and define the language of their representation, enabling the two fields to be acknowledged as separate elements, and not diseases infectious to one other.

Expanding on this viral conflict, particularly between the subjective and objective, in the form of representative language, we must understand that this is a language that mutually connects the two aspects of education and practice like an umbilical cord – a 'give-and-take' connection of mutual dependency on, yet also infection of, one another.

While the dominance of the objective language has revealed the existence of the subjective, this has been at the expense of the subjective's fluent, raw narrative language – now a stereotypical, indoctrinating, misinterpreted, representational language of two-dimensionality. Unfortunately, this has led to the incorrect perception that there is very little difference between the subjective and objective languages, resulting in a refusal to recognise their relation to each other as a virus because, in this case, they achieve a state of stable symbiosis with their sibling host.

However, it is imperative that we define what these two 'representations' are in themselves. While they become images when 'written' or objectively depicted, they still remain images of words already repeated in the mind during thought and, therefore, not images of the things themselves.

Each language is battling with the other, as if that language were reality, and the other illusion, losing sight of the fact that the objective is a symbol in its pictorial or character languages. But despite this, neither language is really a true image.

No matter what the subjective language is, the objective language can immediately be communicated

Education

A year ago, sitting in front of the computer with a bottle of beer next to me, with a constant pressure growing inside me ... a pressure I was unable to define as coming from my tutors or myself, time or perception, imagination or reality ... a pressure of not knowing how to express myself in this 'second language' dialect, or simply the pressure of facing a definition I never had thought about before.

It is true that I had never thought about defining education ... ironic enough because I'd been involved with it for as long as I could remember. Growing up I was around teachers, class mates and inside a room (any kind of room with four white walls and a blackboard) for hours and hours ... but nobody had ever asked me before for any kind of definition, and I had never thought about it because I never needed to ... school was

something I had known from a young age would be the 'ticket' to achieve my dreams ... even when I had no idea what my dreams were. A year ago I needed the beer in order to have the courage to express myself on a blank sheet of paper, to express in words why I couldn't really criticise my education – because I had never realised what it really meant to me.

Text and image: Ana Rute Faisca

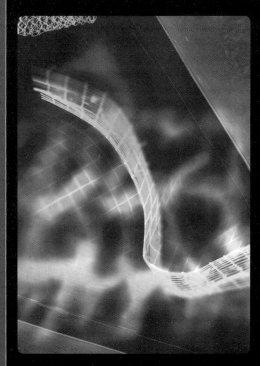

Background

I come from a small country where the mentality of the majority of the people is that anything that comes from abroad is better than what we can do as society, as community or as

individuals. I could try to explain this. However, for me it is one of those things that has no logic and also one of those things that made me want to come to London, imagining that better place, that 'land' of 'great' ideals

– any place outside Portugal where anyone can achieve more than we (the Portuguese people) could ever hope to achieve. The reality is always different ...

text and image: Ana Rute Faisca

in drawing or two-dimensional depiction to anybody from any cultural background; for example, there can be 10 different spoken words for a symbol, yet the symbol remains the same. Thus the subjective language refers to an abjective language – forcing it to be verbalised in auditory patterns – but the objective language does not. In analysing, disassembling and desensitising the automatic verbal reactions to an objective language, it becomes apparent that it is the misunderstanding of the nature of these languages that enables those who manipulate objective languages to control thought on a mass scale within individuals, institutions and society as a whole – and particularly the relationship between practice and education.

There is a need to purify the two languages, and to understand the supporting role of each in relation to the other; a need to work in scrap books translating the connection between subjective thoughts and objective depictions, a need to eradicate the corrupting influence of the objective language upon the subjective – such as text upon thought – so as to be fully efficient and expressive of dreams and the subconscious, and to be able to think for any length of time in images – without words.

An example of this would be the mind's experience of thought when dreaming, listening to music, watching a film or reading pornographic material. These are experiences of thinking in association blocks rather than in basic representational languages. This is the confusion of image (illusion) and thought (reality), where devolution of the idea and thought becoming subservient to the image is necessary to avoid the split of illusion from reality.

It is this confusion of reality with illusion that borders on sending the subject of architecture into a sense of psychosis[1] unless it is diffused. Thus if the dual entity of architecture – spread across the two misinterpreted and, currently, incorrectly defined separate philosophies of education and practice – is allowed to continue, it will develop with the most far-reaching consequences, affecting any sense of identity and disturbing any relationship with the surrounding world. The sense of self is central to an individual subject's whole being and, if this starts to disintegrate it will begin to affect psychological functions such as thought, feeling, action, perception and orientation. This will seriously impair the borders between self and environment. Certainties become uncertainties, the familiar becomes unfamiliar, and the individual topic becomes a stranger to itself.

The topic's existence is thus threatened in a very elementary manner. Perceptive disorders become apparent when the familiar becomes unfamiliar; for example, the difficulty in distinguishing between what is important and what is insignificant. Previously

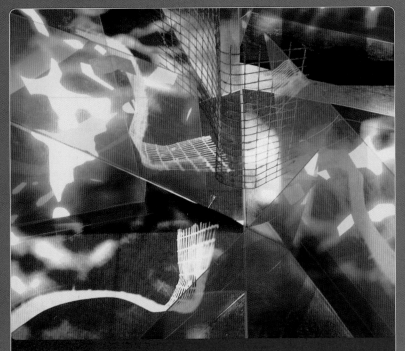

Present Moment

My education in the London was a dream come true. I was doing what I had been dreaming of. However, my extreme ideal of leaving Portugal for a better place was in fact quite different from the reality – but isn't it always like that? Things are never exactly what we expect them to be; they are always different – either better or worse. London South Bank was simply the quickest option to choose. I didn't know a thing about architecture, but what I did know was that I really wanted to learn about it. I came to the university three years ago. I'd never been to a different university, so it is difficult to judge whether or not it would have been better elsewhere. It is certainly more challenging than what I had at high school back in Portugal, which was only theory after boring theory, with no linear logic because I wasn't interested in assimilating all that knowledge without practical output and then having to prove all that in two hours of written exams. I don't feel that I have any kind of experience to comment on what is right or wrong in education; what could be better or worse; what I actually really enjoy in my present education or not, because I know that I need a different experience to appreciate what I have now. But I must say that no country is better than the other, not even in terms of education as I had previously thought. It is simply different.

Text and image: Ana Rute Faisca

Architectural Education

A year later, and here I am again thinking about education, thinking about applying to university again, but thinking why should I? A year later I am working in an office that gives me little of what I'd imagined working would be, but again ... things are always different from how I imagine them to be in the future! Maybe I am just facing what everyone always wonders ... is it for THIS that I have been studying architecture? Is architecture what I really want? I guess that all those conceptual ideals, challenging ideas, creating and destroying patterns, dreaming that there are no limits to the imagination, have so little outcome out here. I guess the gap between education and practice is evident, which makes me wonder why. Why do they have to be such extremes? What is really missing from the dream world (education) and reality (work)? How could both relate to each other for a moderate interaction? I do not know. However, what I do know is that architectural education motivates me to dream, and I am a dreamer. I know that I want to study for the next two years, because I like to dream. Afterwords I will do my best not to wake up again.

Text: Ana Rute Faisca
Image: Jenny Moore

insignificant impressions take on a new and all-important significance. All concept of space and time breaks down, and other elements may appear as having changed in some way, for example becoming distorted or only shadowy forms. The subject of architecture will begin to feel alien with the growth of derealisation and depersonalisation. And thought processes will also undergo a change. The unimportant becomes important. The subject's thought process appears illogical and disjointed to the observer. Not only is the content of the thought itself affected but so, too, is the actual flow of thought, language and word formation.

Delusions are the subject's attempts to give coherency to the incoherencies of its life. They thus function as a defence mechanism. They are a desperate attempt to counteract the disintegration of the self, to repair the cracks in order to maintain a vestige of identity and contact with the surrounding world. If the delusions are doubted by others, inevitably the individual's fear will increase. Hallucinations can also be explained as attempts to make sense of delusions by altering the subject's sense of perception. But these are bound to fail, as they are not in tune with reality. This furthers the loss of contact with the surrounding world, and if this development continues, and the incoherencies, contradictions and fears continue to increase, the subject sees no alternative but to sever communication with the outside world. The subject becomes locked into an internal parallel world of 'otherness' and it becomes increasingly difficult to return to normality.

Thus there is a need to understand that within the subject of architecture there are two bodies, two minds, one soul, each with its own heart to be true to – and this is the infliction of education and practice, 'the conjoined twins of architecture'. Architecture, the subject, is a constant that contains the fields of education and practice. These two fields are not part of a chronological path of verticality, one following the other in a process of cause and effect. In fact, they are two parts of a whole, entwined by birth, yet self-defined, separate individuals – less than 'father and son', more than brothers. Not twins either – more 'peas in a pod' existing along a horizontal line of thought. One is not subservient to the other, but neither are they equals, and they cannot coexist nor function adequately or to their full potential until this is realised. Education and practice are conjoined (Siamese) twins. They are inseparable as they are both physically and mentally entwined and in the intolerable position of can't live with, yet definitely can't live without one another. They therefore need to be respected as separate individuals by their own personalities.

So how is it that we, as individuals, function within this 'split personality' of architecture and its separate fields? How are we meant to be responsible to the subject of architecture and the role of architect creator, whether as practitioners or educators? The answer is, as individuals in our own right – in not succumbing to this schitzophrenic parallel world, but maintaining the individual questioning of our minds, ignoring the burden of the term 'architect' and, instead, being responsible to ourselves and not the institutions. There is a need to rebel, not revolt, against the current situation if we are to succeed.

It is therefore necessary to establish that in the role of creator, we are observers, and not citizens of, society. As individuals we are bound to explore every aspect of human experience – the good, the bad and the ugly – sometimes unconditionally, as well as the dark and perverse aspects of the human condition, including our own. We cannot worry about what our own segment of society considers good or bad behaviour, exploration, interpretation and presentation. Thus one cannot be a creator and a citizen at the same time, which makes it clear that we have no social responsibility whatsoever.

When we must be the citizen, step back and see what happens, examine why we have an impulse to create and show the things that put us in a different position, we're no longer being a creator but an analyst of the act itself. (However, we must acknowledge that there are many creators who do not feel the need to examine process, or who fear that if they do it will disappear, alter or affect them beyond reproach.) So we could say in the same breath that we are citizens and that we do, in fact, have social responsibilities, and we do take that seriously. But we must also be aware that as an artist, our responsibility is to allow ourselves complete freedom. This is our purpose, what we're here for.

We need to be aware that the coexistence between society and art is an uneasy one. If art is anti-repression, then art and civilisation were not meant for each other. You don't have to be freudian to see that. The pressure in the unconscious – the voltage – is to be heard, to express. It is irrepressible, and will find a way out.

When we create or analyse we produce, and we must not censor our own imagery or our connections. We must not worry about what critics will say, what statutory bodies will say, what environmentalists will say, or what the institutions within which we exist will say. We must ignore all of this. If we listen to all those opinions and unasked-for advice we will be paralysed. We have to go back to the voice that spoke before all of these strictures were imposed on it, and let it speak these terrible truths. By being irresponsible we will be responsible.

Once one looks deeper into what social responsibility really means, one inevitably ends

> When we create or analyse we produce, and we must not censor our own imagery or connections. We must not worry about what critics will say, what statutory bodies will say, what environmentalists will say or what the institutions within which we exist will say. We must ignore all of this.

up examining personal responsibility. You don't have one without the other. If you're trying to consider something pure and innate, as opposed to just culturally relative, you have to delve deep within yourself, which can be perilous.

So in the realm of architecture do we, as individuals, have a huge responsibility because of the projects we create? And if so, how are we to bear the weight of that responsibility? Our projects are good for the people. It is not intended that they are created simply to support or encourage a certain philosophy. The project doesn't do anything. It just hangs or sits there waiting to be engaged with.

So is it the creator, the critic, the teacher or the occupier who possesses the right to say, for example, whether a project is good, that they approve of it, partake in it? Where does this come from? If it's to be a true art form, it is conceivable that the author him- or herself, and others involved in the project, do not in the process of developing it know exactly what the project is saying. They don't know what the project is supporting or expressing. It's in the process of making that you begin to come to some understanding of this. Therefore, you cannot have a group of people amongst the entrails of a project at mere initial concept stage for its meaning, social significance, political correctness, etc. Ultimately that's nonsense.

So does anyone have the balance, the magisterial cosmic perspective that means he or she can look at a project and say: 'This is irresponsible and must be suppressed'? In reality there are only little committees of scared, timid people who are fumbling around in this respect. But if such a God-like person did exist, some kind of accepted arbitrator, someone who could say to us: 'Hey! I know you don't think such a project is going to enhance such and such in society but I, God, tell you that in the light of the next 2,000 years it will,' then maybe we could submit to that arbitration. But still we must continue to refuse to be suppressed.'[2] ⌂

'I want to show the unshowable, speak the unspeakable.'
— David Cronenberg

Notes
1 The explanation and definitions of psychosis explained within this article originate, and are heavily borrowed from, Dr Peter Schopf's text 'Psychoses'.
2 This full text is copied and adapted from the chapter 'Bugs, Spies and Butterflies' in Cronenberg on Cronenberg, edited by Chris Rodley.

Kevin Rhowbotham

Kevin Rhowbotham is a unique phenomenon in education. Outspoken, he delivers a constant critique of the architectural establishment's limitations. Never short of an opinion, he is also never shy to give an opinion. Here he produces a text on teaching, with images by Jonathan Nicholls, relating to concerns on education and its media representations.

The end of empty formalism

In some quarters there was, at one time at least, a concerned conceptualism within teaching. I am thinking now of the work of Peter Smithson, of Cedric Price and of David Green. But this was always and already surrounded by a formalist fog. These guys were the politicos of their extended generation. Around them, a miasma of vacuity obscured their attempts to establish some irony, inversion and critique of the current situation.

Fifteen years ago it seemed entirely useful to pull out some inferences from a general return to Kantian formalism and to pursue the possibilities of a predominantly expatriate French taste for the wholly formal, albeit tainted with Marxist intentions. Following Derrida and Foucault, as many struggled to do before discovering Giles Deleuze, a formal critique seemed a good idea, at least at the time, but it proved, eventually, far too politically muscular for a profession already weaned on the pacifying effects of inoffensive style. Better to shed the political bite of poststructuralist deconstruction, and build your own; and the more formally uncontrollable it appeared the more adulation it seemed to receive. As for concept, there was certainly very little room to rethink the inadvertency of this formalist gush.

The resident conservatism of all architecture schools leaves them ill-equipped to counter the general drift of the architectural avant-garde and completely powerless to oppose it, no matter how ludicrous its intentions. Diploma schools operate a mute plagiarism by default, having no means by which they might launch or sustain a research position. The result has been a myopic and reactionary formalism, most dramatically in evidence at the Bartlett school, divorced from the complex and pleural demands of the present. There is nowhere in Britain, other than at the AA itself, any talk of programme, of pertinent use, and of the contemporary relevance of things. All things are concerned with process and with surface, issues surely dead and buried 15 years ago.

Many troubled countenances reflect upon the nature of the work of these formalist schools without really understanding precisely why they are troubled. The problem is not one of irrelevance to the pragmatism of professional practice.

Teaching must be for itself and be cut against the pertinent concerns of contemporary culture. Why so many people are dumbly troubled by formalism is that it has had its day; it has failed to deliver a pertinent critique of contemporary architectural practice.
Several ironies illuminate the darker landscapes of teaching, and by no means the least is that which makes its practice more instructive and certainly more spiritually fulfilling than its reception.

If you want to learn, then teach, as the pious saying goes.

The trouble is, what you can learn – if you really want to teach, and if you want to teach with spirit, not to say love – isn't architecture. Mother architecture is merely the white whore of geometry. Teaching architecture is an exercise in the limits of thinking and, as such, begins with a question and with the construction of a criticism. To say so much is already to reveal an inner truth too potent for the rank and vile.

Plurality

Written by a Doctor in Plain Words

THE **Positions** OF **Architecture** IN BUILDING

because--

—there are different positions that can be taken in architecture, and it is desirable that the position should be varied just as often as fancy may chance to dictate. Variety in building technique, as in other things in life, adds a certain spice that need not be refused for any reason known to common sense.

INDEPENDENCE

THE WORLD CAN BE YOURS

become a person with dominant strength, courage of independence and self-sufficiency. Resist being dependant upon any power outside your own.

What your new found architectural enthusiasm does for your Physiologically

1. Aids digestion.
2. Improves metabolism.
3. Relieves tension.
4. Improves muscle function.
5. Stimulates circulation.
6. Steps up endocrine action (hormones).
7. Stabilises the blood pressure.
8. Stimulates a dynamo of energy.
9. Provides a feeling of euphoria (well-being).
10. Establishes reserve power for periods when you are feeling low.

Those Questions That Blast Many Projects —Answered Fearlessly and Frankly!

ARCHITECTURE SCHOOL

Without cost or obligation, please send me a copy of your 48-page booklet, "Making Beautiful Buildings." I am most interested in learning:

☐ How to Plan and Make Attractive Clothes
☐ How to Earn Money Designing for Others
☐ How to Become a Professional Architect
☐ How to Design and Make Becoming Buildings
☐ How to Become a Successful Architect
☐ The Art of Successful Architecture

Name ....
(Please specify whether Mr, Mrs or Miss)

Address ....

cultures and which have finally become a basic component of the human species.

These are, for example, the following:

That there are enduring things;

That architecture might endure or be more than an ephemeral and fleeting condition;

That there are identical things;

That architecture might gain value by association;

That there are things, material, bodies;

That the categories of material and rational definition are complete and describe the world of architecture completely;

That there are things which retain meanings inherently in so far as they appear to be what they are;

That the value of things derives from their usefulness;

That our willing is free;

That what is good for me, is good in itself.

These stand as permanent impediments to free thought and must be overcome by the diligent teacher attempting to love her students. ∞

Jonathan Hill

Jonathan Hill, director of the ground-breaking MPhil/PhD in architectural design at the Bartlett School of Architecture, discusses the history of researching, testing and questioning architecture through the media of drawing and writing.

Educated

At Nanjing Institute of Technology (now Southeast University), Nanjing, China
In the very first architecture class I entered after the Great Cultural Revolution in 1978, any ideological content, and even the notion of design, were avoided. It was a training in building technology.

At Ball State University, Indiana, US
Although the curriculum at Ball State would be considered as mainstream American, conceptual thinking was rigorously introduced in the studio by a visiting professor from the AA in London.

At the University of California at Berkeley, US
The debate between design and social concerns stirred up a keen awareness of the purposes of architecture among students, and tremendous confusion as to why design and society are in opposition.

Educating (Past Tense)

At Ball State University, University of Michigan, University of California at Berkeley, and Rice University, Texas, US
After working briefly in architects' offices in San Francisco, I began my teaching career as an assistant professor at Ball State and later went on to other institutions of higher education in the US for a period of 11 years, from 1985 to 1996. As I developed an intense interest in conceptual thinking, my pedagogical interest was focused on the quest for architectural ideas concerning space and programme or time and experience, often with an interdisciplinary dimension. Film, installation, literature, painting and other art media were examined and brought into, or overlapped on to, the architectural discourse or used simply as analytical and/or representational tools.

Design was defined as a process of search and research, and pursued as a methodological and theoretical endeavour. Building may or may not have been the end product. In fact, process was frequently emphasised over product. The conventions of problem solving and case study in the design studio were critically questioned and challenged. Therefore, the design of studio problems was considered crucial for teaching, and carefully conceived to acknowledge the complexity of design thinking and to avoid reducing the exercises to a repetitive, merely skill-polishing routine. For example, while at Rice University, reading JG Ballard's science-fiction Crash was juxtaposed with observation

of highways in Houston in an attempt to fully discover the motor-happy urbanism of America. Site, programme and architectural design were all determined by the students according to their individual comprehension of both the novel and the city.

Looking back, I was a part of a radical experiment in design pedagogy which, in the 1980s, nurtured a subculture in the American academia of architecture. However, such an approach to teaching tends to emphasise the artistic and the creative, whilst overlooking the social and the practical, sometimes creating a distance from reality.

Educating (Present Tense)

At Peking University, Beijing
When I was given the opportunity of establishing a new programme of architecture at Peking University in 1999, I had been practising in China for the past seven years. As my position shifted to a practitioner/educator, I was able to perceive both the profession and the education from what was, for me, a previously unthinkable standpoint. Architecture can remain a discipline relevant to contemporary life and culture if the gap between theory and practice, or the academic and the social, is bridged. There cannot be an either/or choice between society and design. It has to be the same architecture for both the school and the profession. It has to be social responsibilities fulfilled through design, the best or most advanced architectural design possible.

Architectural education is confronted by the same issues as the rest of the field – if not the world – from

technology to ecology, from consumerism to regionalism, as well as from urbanisation to globalisation. The school is obliged to investigate, to probe, to experiment with possible solutions or sometimes alternative ones, in order to lead, to redefine or to revive the profession. The school thus has to refuse any simple mode of production.

Specifically for China, recognising a perplexing tradition of painterly-oriented Beaux-Arts education, and an overwhelming pressure from a skyrocketing market economy, the newly established school, the Peking University Graduate Center of Architecture, is forced to take on the challenge from both the academic realm as well as the broader reality. Strategically, we have devised a three-year masters' curriculum of two architectures: one autonomous, one social.

The study of autonomous architecture is the focus of the first-year Tectonic Studio, where students design and build either a small functional facility, such as a wood workshop or meeting/reading room, or a space for pure pedagogical purposes, such as a Space-study Apparatus. Students have the constraint of a small budget and must calculate both the construction cost and the structural loads. Managing the budget and the schedule is as important as the act of erecting the building. Drawings can be made only when the need occurs. This is an architecture that is physically assembled and intimately experienced. Since its every detail is meant to be resolved, this architecture could be myopic. Thus, it is also the micro studio.

The study of social architecture takes place in the second-year Urban Studio, where students research various conditions of Chinese urbanisation, focusing mainly on Beijing as a case study. City is seen as a complex organism of political, economic, social and cultural forces supported by the organisation of material resources, including space. The spatial structure of Beijing has been documented and analysed in terms of visual experience and planning intentions. The evolution of enclosure in the city, from courtyard house to work-unit compound to gated community, is traced as physical evidence of the social changes in modern Chinese history. The present planning codes, such as daylight distance, floor area ratio, building coverage, greenery coverage and setback, are decoded rather as a vision for an anti-city, since the collective result of these requirements denies coherent urban spaces and encourages the building of objects. It is hoped that students may

Right, top and bottom
Tectonic Studio, Peking University Graduate Center of Architecture, 2002
Individual Space-Study Apparatus is the name of a building that measures 3 metres long by 3 metres wide and 4 metres high. Four students designed and built it by themselves. The structure carries the movement of an individual and interacts with him or her, since it is a piece of moving architecture. The rectangular box is divided into two equal parts. One half has wheels, which enable it to slide on the rails installed in the ground and alter its relative position to the other half. The sliding movement brings changes to space, light and paths. The design suggests the notion of game and play, and may seem useless. The designers/builders hope that one may be in the apparatus doing nothing, or that it can be redefined in as many ways as one wishes. For example, it was almost used as the stage for a rock band.

establish their own social agenda through urban studies whilst developing an understanding of the phenomenon of city. This is the learning of greater architecture and thus the macro studio.

Peking University resists traditional design assignment, which mocks social practice by creating building proposals for fictitious sites and programmes. One of the reasons for this is that the university admits students in architecture who typically go through a five-year undergraduate programme, which offers case-study-based design studios across all of the levels. More fundamentally, it is believed that, at graduate level in present-day China, it is more important to improve the ability to identify and comprehend architectural issues than to develop design skills.

The third year of our programme gives the student the freedom to complete an independent work, which can be a design thesis, research report or other creative project.

In recent years, the micro and macro studios have also been conducted in other institutions. At Harvard University I taught a third-year graduate studio, the theme of which was 'Beijing Urbanism'. The workshop dealt with the increased density and morphological changes of the city's urban fabric. As devices of the methodology, analysis and design were not consequential but overlapped. Design was engaged as an analytical tool, and analysis as a form of design. A nonlinear process was generated and, when all the stages were compiled together they became the outcome.

At Tongji University in Shanghai I am currently teaching a fourth-year undergraduate studio tackling the 'Problem of 1:2'. All the drawings, including floor plan, section, elevation and interior perspective, for a 30-square-metre exhibition pavilion in a park are to be in 1:2 scale. The attempt is to focus on materiality and construction without involving students in the actual building. Students have to look for materials, think construction methods and reinvent the drafting tools. In addition, students are asked to work on the same sheet of paper throughout, as if building and rebuilding a two-dimensional structure, blurring the line between presentation and representation.

From (studio) problem design to programme design, teaching has been, for me, a process of learning. Perhaps education, similar to design, can only be defined as a journey of search and research. Behind such a definition is the ideal that architecture is essential for the betterment of human conditions – and this is what ought to be delivered to the students. ∆

Right, top and bottom
Lu Xiang, Beijing – Yuan City, Urban Studio, Peking University Graduate Center of Architecture, 2002
In Beijing, 'yuan', or 'courtyard'
in its approximate translation, is always a clearly enclosed and introverted space. The buildings that surround or occupy a yuan are less significant than the yuan in terms of urban formation. The urban spatial structure of Beijing consists of multiple layers of yuan in a three-tiered construction of house-compound-city. Yuan is the basic and consistent element of Beijing's fabric, thus Beijing can be considered a yuan city. However, when yuan is a compound, it may accommodate rich and complex programmes, ranging from office and housing to retail and cultural facilities. In this case a yuan is itself a city or a city within a city.

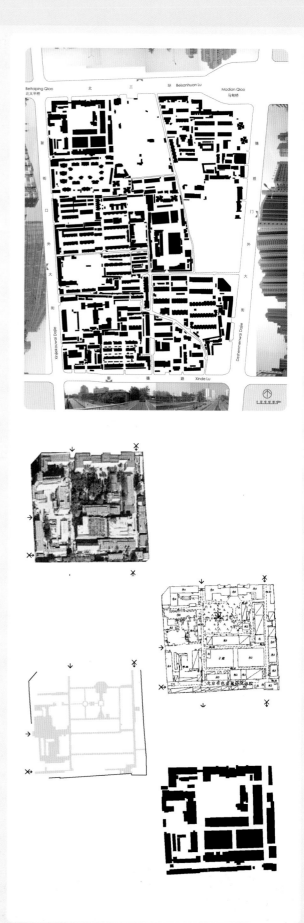

Over the past decade, South Africa has been a country in flux with political change and rebirth. **Lindsay Bremner, David Dewar** and **Iain Low** each explain the current opinions and theoretical positions in their schools and in their homeland.

Iain Low

Iain Low discusses space and transformation in educating architects within the post-apartheid era.

'In a society which holds that no universal truths are possible, nothing is absolute. Therefore, in the end – they say – objective goodness and evil no longer really matter. Good comes to mean what is pleasing or useful at a particular moment.
Evil means what contradicts our subjective wishes. Each person can build a private system of values.'
— Pope John Paul II,Denver, Colorado, 1993

Space
Space, and therefore architecture, as the physical manifestation of a set of power relations should form a central focus in South Africa's agenda for transformation. In implementing the spatial agenda of apartheid, the built-environment professions could be considered to have been the handmaidens of the Afrikaner Nationalist government. The policy of 'setting apart' was realised through purposeful acts of spatial discrimination. In fulfilling this, personal interest and professional expertise were immorally allied in constructing the apartheid legacy of racialised urbanism. Characterised predominantly by segregation, this phenomenon continues to identify the South African landscape.

In this era of late Western capitalism, fewer architectural practitioners are interested in the architectural project as a mode of enquiry. For most professionals, architecture seems to be a commercial endeavour, whereby product, efficiency and economic utilitarianism govern the mode of production. An emergent space, defining

the interrelationship between the academy and the profession, seemingly parallels the gap between the richest and poorest members of our society, making the task of design education more provocative.

Notwithstanding the above, the project of architecture and, more particularly, the final design project for the BArch degree at the University of Cape Town (UCT) present fertile ground for the building of critical difference by questioning and developing individual design character and capacity.

Topical Thinking
Topical thinking frames the discourse in the thesis/major-project bachelor of architecture programme at UCT. Although 'design discourse' in the department is directed at independent enquiry, current investigations by thesis candidates tend to reflect events and concerns in the contemporary South African city. The city, as perhaps the highest form of built human expression, therefore becomes a natural locus for speculation and thinking topically. Despite a predominance of inner-city situations, individual topics are individually identified through a process of research and the discourse around issues of transformation in relation to emerging political processes,[1] simultaneously grounded by contemporary architectural theory.

Hybridity
Hybridity, and the 'critique of type' within the limitations of its assumptions of certainty, finds obvious resonance in the South African context. Whereas in the past certainty prevailed, indeterminacy has now come to rule. Consequently, in the absence of any regulating framework, the prospect is for students to negotiate an architectural position. By mediating their inner

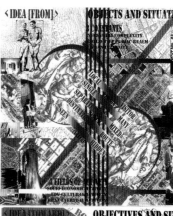

Right
Sadiq Toffa, 'Meeting Dialogue:
Informing the Commons of
Dialogue', BArch, 2003
This project seeks the informed
coexistence of the city with the
Bo-Kaap, a predominantly
Muslim neighbourhood that
'survived' the onslaught of
apartheid. Through a thoughtful
urban strategy, the project
sought to establish comfortable
ground for the meeting of the
differences that exemplify the
post-apartheid South African city,
particularly between disparate
urban communities. The
architectural insertions project
an imagery that contributes a
new layer of urbanity in which
original modes of production and
form are reinterpreted. These in
turn afford a contemporary
reading of the post-apartheid city
and posit a transformed tectonic
and imagery.

Bottom left
Craig McClenaghan, The
EveryDay and the Celebrated:
investigating appropriate
architectural interventions for
the cultural and spatial
consequences of urban burial
at Philippi interchange', Cape
Town, BArch, 2002
This project responds to the
growing demand for land that
has resulted from the AIDS crisis
in southern Africa. Speculating
upon a number of projected
scenarios, the scheme attempts
to offer a contemporary solution
to Xhosa burial practice.

Bottom right
Dieter Brandt, 'Locating
Displacement: Re-presenting
Difference', BArch, 2002
This investigation addressed the
problem presented by urban
abandonment and transitional
instability. Attempting to identify
an appropriate architectural
intervention to bring together
seemingly disparate agendas of
migrants, refugees and local
community, placed the author in
direct confrontation with the
extremes of contemporary
difference. Mapping the terrain
identified invisible fields
constructed by the power
relations of competing interests
of displaced peoples;
druglordism, youth and taxi
drivers. Para-siting on to the
public rail authority became the
only rational act of resistance
through which to re-present
multiple and competing interests.

Notes
1 National Government's
Green/White Paper policy
positions contribute significant
input to research
2 Observe the formal similitude
across the 'winners' in the RIBA
President's medallists. Despite
their apparently diverse enquiries,
programmes and siting contexts,
formal continuity persists.

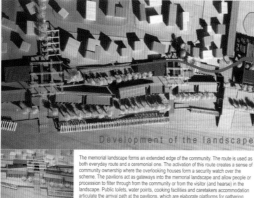

Development of the landscape

The memorial landscape forms an extended edge of the community. The route is used as both everyday route and a ceremonial one. The activation of this route creates a sense of community ownership where the overlooking houses form a security watch over the scheme. The pavilions act as gateways into the memorial landscape and allow people or procession to filter through from the community or from the visitor (and hearse) in the landscape. Public toilets, water points, cooking facilities and caretakers accommodation articulate the arrival path at the pavilions, which are elaborate platforms for gathering.

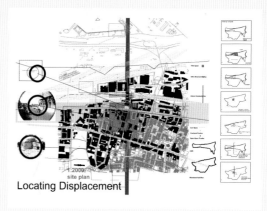

Locating Displacement

subjectivity with the collective consciousness of their situation, critical differences emerge as students engage in a project to 'rewrite type' through their individual enquiry.

Method: Rewriting Type –
Issue/Siting/Programming

The indiscrete influence of both precedent and the linear 'date/place/building' method promoted by conventional conceptions of architectural history demands direct confrontation. However, conversely, with the demise of the metanarrative, it seems that any arbitrary offering has become possible. Consequently, design as process characterises architectural thinking at UCT.

Firstly, 'taking issue' demands the formulation of a defensible design position that sponsors a grounded enquiry. Site and programme are then interpreted as verbs demanding a researched and argued uncovering of 'siting and programming' as core design generators. These issues are individually motivated and reinterpreted through a 'narrative process' whereby interactive exercises seek to provoke difference and affect the new sets of social arrangements necessary for the construction of hybrids. Process becomes privileged above that of final product. The hegemony of material culture and its formal consequences is thereby contested. Social dialogue and the possibility associated with temporality have become checks for identifying a thoughtful and resilient material culture within architectural enquiry. In this sense, 'form' is subjugated and our students' architectural products do not necessarily compete comfortably with the 'anaesthetic sex appeal' seemingly promoted by global practice and education alike.[2]

In responding to this circumstance, students individually construct an ethical base from which to operate and intervene in the city. Architectural language becomes personal, and whilst their building type and physical arrangements may seem less familiar, the human conditions addressed are iterative. Situations of living/working/recreating/learning/interacting, and so on persist, and it becomes possible to empower the concerns of these ordinary rituals in formalising both the everyday and the celebratory in human life.

Lindsay Bremner

At the University of Witwatersrand in Johannesburg, **Lindsay Bremner** has redirected the gaze of the architecture school towards its immediate surroundings - a vibrant, teeming city in flux.

My tenure as chair of architecture at the University of the Witwatersrand in Johannesburg for the last six years has been compelled by engagement with the city in which the school is situated. Johannesburg – abrasive, collapsing, colliding, iconoclastic, a rapidly changing city in a rapidly transforming society. Not 15 years ago, it was a smug, self-contained, medium-sized colonial city of some 350,000 inhabitants – all white – whose architectures deferred to the metropolitan centres of the UK or US. Today it is a teeming African metropolis of nearly 4 million – fluid, messy, contested, violent. A city where the global is being staked out, marked by new presences, new modalities of occupying, making and traversing space that often overlay, intersect with and contradict the (sub) urban fragmentations of its apartheid past.

What do these contestations – these transgressions – mean for architecture and for architectural education? Does it simply repel them, retreating into the comfort zones of an accredited curriculum, professional liability or good taste? Or does it try to understand, theorise and incorporate them into a new conception of what architecture is and does? Does it have instruments, tools through which to engage with this city-in-the-making and negotiate its emerging spaces? How does one build the architecture(s) of this unsettled city? What are its models, and what are its modes?

First attempts to address these questions admitted the practices and aesthetic of the 'informal' into the spectre of the architectural gaze. How street traders, illegal immigrants, informal settlement dwellers and suburban developers negotiate and make space became the reference for the architectural imagery. Could architecture intervene in these spaces? Could they provide the clues for new ways of imagining and making?

This work produced not new metanarratives for the post-apartheid city, but a collection of little works, responding to the fragile social and economic practices through which people were engaging with the problematic of living in the post-apartheid city. They were not only architectural works, but also a form of critical discourse on the (formal) city and its limits.

This approach is not new. Its legacy stretches back to Aldo van Eyck's postwar children's playgrounds in Amsterdam, to JB Jackson's fascination for the ordinary, working-class American landscape, to the work of Venturi and Scott Brown. More recently Lebbeus Woods' Wild City project in San Sperato and Teddy Cruz's work with students on the US Mexican border, by questioning the stability of given categories – architect/nonarchitect, inside/outside, centre/periphery, urban/rural, global/local, formal/informal – exposed the assumptions, collusions and intersections of power/knowledge in which both architecture and the city were held. Architecture becomes a way of negotiating these boundaries.

This redirecting of the architectural gaze has had a number of consequences on our way of teaching and our curriculum. The conventions of the studio and the crit have been stretched around new worlds. A new curriculum, teaching architectural history from an African perspective, has revealed the impossibility of thinking history consequentially. Two 'all-school projects' have allowed students to interrogate the city and its consequences for architecture outside of the parameters of the regular curriculum, punctuating its rhythm with another set of learning rituals. The design-build studio has emerged as an important mode for engagement with the city and its processes, extending the conventions of the architectural studio into the public realm – the city itself.

Above right
'At Home and Away', all-school project, 2000
Model of housing prototype for the city's homeless. Students interrogating the meaning of home and homelessness for Johannesburg's marginal city dwellers – refugees, illegal immigrants, street dwellers, informal settlers – and how we, as architects, might engage with them. This produced a number of installations and exhibits, modelling new imageries of city life.

David Dewar

David Dewar defines how the balance of values, knowledge and skills missing from the architectural education profession may be readdressed.

Architecture as a profession is consistently declining in status internationally. The reasons for this rest almost entirely with the discipline itself. Four reasons, in particular, underpin this trend.

The first is that architecture has increasingly become the handmaiden of the rich and, particularly, the large property developer, as opposed to society at large. It is the values of greed that most commonly inform outcomes, and the relevance of the profession to society is increasingly questioned.

The second is that the discipline has become obsessed with form and technology. It is the images in the glossy magazines that increasingly dominate both student and professional thinking, as opposed to fundamental concerns about space, structure, light and air.

The third is that its focus has increasingly become the object – the (usually) freestanding building – as opposed to the role of the building in a broader context. This is especially true in relation to urban settlements. The role of the discipline in contributing to improved urban performance, and particularly the quality of the public spatial environment, has become increasingly marginalised.

Finally, in the face of the ever-increasing professional specialisation in the field of the built environment, the discipline has allowed its role to become increasingly narrowly defined.

A return to relevance demands two fairly radical shifts – shifts which by definition must begin with architectural education.

The first is returning to an emphasis on thinking from first principles, based firmly on the two ethical pillars of humanism and environmentalism.

The concern with humanism recognises that the real clients of any architectural or urban design project are the common people upon whom the project impacts, including generations yet unborn. Good design is based on the creative satisfaction of human need. Positive change requires that architecture reacknowledges its social role and relevance

in placing before society new and better possibilities for meeting human need in the field of the built environment. To do this, it is necessary to acknowledge the normative basis of the discipline and to grapple consciously with the spatial implications of values such as equity, social justice, integration and dignity, for these are the issues of our time.

At the heart of the concern with environmentalism are the concepts of sustainability and place: architectural education needs to address these directly.

The second shift requires a conscious recognition of the context of architecture, particularly the city. Improved urban performance is the collective responsibility of all of the professions concerned with the built environment. It can be achieved only through much greater interdisciplinary approaches (involving the examination of a shared problem definition from different disciplinary perspectives) as opposed to multidisciplinary approaches (different professions, often with different agendas and interpretations of the problem working on the same issue), which are currently the norm. To achieve this requires the conscious blurring of disciplinary boundaries which, in turn, requires a broadening of the base of architectural education, while at the same time deepening and sharpening core competencies.

At the heart of sound architectural education is achieving a balance between values/knowledge/skills. It is the issue of values that has been most eroded. Without these for direction, architectural judgement simply reduces to opinion: increasingly, there is not even the basis for vigorous debate and argument, which is the revitalising lifeblood of any discipline. ◭

Above right
Scheme by Tariq Toffa, University of Cape Town, 2002
The scheme deals with the difficult issue of integrating group-specific facilities into the urban fabric. The site forms an interface between the Bo-Kaap (a predominantly Muslim residential area) and the central business district of Cape Town. Local group-specific facilities (for example, a madrassa) are inserted into the hollow centre of an existing residential block, as opposed to relating to the commonly shared public space of the city centre.

Vladislav & Luidmila Kirpichev

Vladislav and Luidmila Kirpichev work innovatively with children at EDAS, their non-state architecture school in Moscow. Inspired by the ideas of Wolf Prix, the confrontation of anarchy has become integral to their ideas and working methodology.

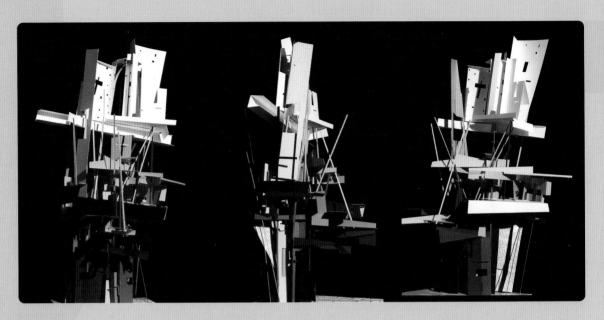

The EDAS school is not about the children, but how to learn from them. Founded in 1977, it has never pretended to be a school for children, but one for the consolidation of young antagonists, artists, film makers – and architects.

Since we set up EDAS and began presenting children's work, people have been expecting us to release information about our work formula that would explain the phenomenon of its success for us. These kids' untrained output achieves a truly extraordinary professionalism, their pieces reaching such a high standard that we wouldn't have believed it possible if we hadn't witnessed it with our own eyes. The individuality they display in the approach to and execution of their work is not governed by any kind of external influences but is triggered instead by their own spontaneous input – nothing except their own raw will and emotions. Actually, in terms of the kids we worked with, it seemed we had to deal with an absolutely blank sheet, one without preconceptions or a hidden agenda. Their non-knowledge helped them to be independent and behave radically, and the resultant abstraction very quickly became our main language of communication.

In 1986 we were commissioned by the then Ministry of Education of the Soviet Union to create a methodological manual for countrywide distribution. Stimulated by the idea, we went to work with great enthusiasm, but soon discovered that the best, and only, advice we could actually give in the light of our EDAS experience was: 'Don't tell them what to do!'

We did, however, try again, some 15 years ago. This time we were asked to produce a book about EDAS. We have continued the process right up to the present, so it now has more than 2,000 pages with 3,500 (selected!)

Opening page
'Sources of Anarchy in Architecture', studio with students from Wolf D Prix's class at the University of Applied Arts Vienna, 2003–04.

Right and above
Ivan K, age 10, 1994. The object is a combination of its fragments without any logic in the connection of them all. Coloured paper and cardboard. Height: 75 centimetres.

images, but as it is an influx analysis of a constantly evolving and redefined process, we are still not in a position to present finite conclusions or a definitive summary. Thus the book grows larger and larger, and each page starts with an excited, 'Look, that's happened!' and finishes 'and don't do the same!'. This has taught us that we should never try to theorise our experience, because it's changing all the time, with no beginning or end.

So there is no exact prescription for the process, it's never defined: the kids are told to try everything – analysing and taking steps backwards and forwards – altering, reconsidering, improving – to start from scratch and try something else – collage and perhaps reorganising the sense of the piece – backwards

burgeoning artistic judgement. This allows them the confidence to step forward and stand alone against tradition and popular opinion.

To get to this position there are quite a number of exercises. There are lessons once a week, for instance three hours in the studio, where the kids have to fulfil tasks in a rolling 15-minute set of deadlines. The technique is always different – drawings, models, paintings, collages; and at the end of the day they each have accumulated a minimum of 12 projects which range from the sweet to the sweaty, because without knowing it they are in constant competition, not only with one another but also with themselves.

For the next seven days, the students live with seven different tasks – one for each day, with different estimated duration times, from 15 minutes to five hours. While the tutor could simply control the time, it

and forwards – again and again – being completely absurd and contradictory – cut – glue – destroy etc. As they evolve, the more they are initially displeased with their process, progress and production. The kids are continually abstracting themselves while they are more and more stochastic in a process that is very far from temporal evolution, governed by a kind of weighted randomness that can be chosen to give anything from an entirely determined outcome to an entirely unpredictable one. What later emerges, but not before a certain amount of doubt has arisen as a result of their intense concentration on their projects, is the development of their own rules, which they are simultaneously prompted to subvert by their own

is sometimes down to the students as to how long they spend on each task; the amount they learn is in direct proportion to how they control their time. They may be asked to spend 30 minutes for a phase of a project, which would entail working fast – the idea would be presented very clearly. But initially this is simply the development of working skills – a facility to provide a quick reaction for a task resolution and so hone their intellectual and decision-making abilities.

For us as tutors, it is primarily thanks to Wolf D Prix, who was the first to confront us with the question of anarchy during our studio in his class in Vienna, that we suddenly realised that this is exactly what we have been doing all our lives – confronting anarchy – a strange situation for us as Russians, for whom anarchy and revolution are ingrained within our historic tradition.

Above
Egor K, age 8, 1994. The tower was constructed within 30 minutes from the pieces Egor found around him: without surprises. Its round form was dictated by the roll of paper he was unable to stretch.

It must be made clear that we have absolutely no intention of doing anything comparable with the so-called anarchitecture of Gordon Matta Clark or towards formulating some kind of theory of 'self-urbanism'. Nor do we simply want to contrast the subject with the action and then keep focusing on the process of creating specific conditions, merely for the sake of creating an unpredictable result where unpredictability becomes the be-all and end-all. Each step and each conclusion is a very personal measure of the student's responsibility for his or her work. Our process aims to address all the problems encountered in terms of the problems of meaning, the problems of reality – all the real problems!

This is when anarchy becomes a method – not in order to celebrate opposition for its own sake, but to ignore it, especially when formalism also becomes a tool, because imitation remains the biggest antonym, the biggest enemy of spontaneous creativity. It is the dynamic contrast between these two elements, between the anarchic and the formulaic, that creates movement back from tradition and forward to change. The combination of these two, anarchy (as an intellectual game) + formalism (as the contradiction of imitation), creates the basic skeleton for improvement whereby formalism becomes an analytical method by using such terms as morphology and evolution. This leads to our other important principle: there are no stylistic privileges for anyone and there is no way anyone can expect to just do what they like, whether teacher or pupil or critic.

So for us: 'To educate is to bring up young persons' is the dictionary's definition. However, 'I don't know why they say young persons only – I think old persons should be brought up educated too,' wrote John Hejduk, who continues, 'to give intellectual and moral training, systematic instruction, development of character and mental power.' Although it is considered that age is the important trigger this is not really so, it just leads to different types of conversation. For instance, we'd never explain any examples when we are working with children and never point out what is good or bad in our point of view. We don't want them to know too much before they make their own discoveries. We especially don't want them to rely on anyone else's opinion, as it would mean that their education was limited to an understanding of their own privileges and condition.

This led us, the tutors, to make some important discoveries of our own: however much we have tried to force the kids to make key discoveries for themselves, we couldn't teach them space and colour perception, and they couldn't 'learn' it. We found that every individual has his or her private colour vision, with variety of colour combination being highly dependent on individual interpretation. Whatever you would try, they would always combine the colour in a way they think works and ignore your advice. This was perfect for us. To try to force or change these highly personal aspects could only result

Above and right
Marcus F, student at the University of Applied Science, Frankfurt, summer 1993. This was our first workshop – a very strange transformation of traditional meta-symbols (landscape) into traditional meta-knowledge (building).

Opposite
Egor K, age 9, 1995. Tower project during workshop with the students at the University of Applied Science, Frankfurt, 1995. Red painted wood.Height: 75 centimetres.

in the same outcome as trying to teach someone left-handed to operate with their right hand. As with colour, so with space – one cannot stipulate a 'right' or 'wrong' spatial awareness – it's a very personal question.

To ask the question 'Why?' in relation to their work will only drive a student down a dead end. Yet actually the question 'Why?' is a vital motor of education: how to define and in what context to use it; get the context wrong and it can undermine everything. It reminds us of the scenario when we once struggled to explain the meaning of the term 'axonometric' to a five- to six-year-old. Well, it took us just three minutes once we had hit upon the right approach. That scenario established for us that discussions have a quintessential ending, and that's why we stopped seeing our actions as teaching and rather as a process of negotiation. So, in working with the students, our view was no longer to expect them to be just a 'blank piece of paper' but to be prepared for them to be ready to analyse their previous experiences in order to escape the banality of architectural education and instead push the arguments to their extreme.

And this leads us to our next vital principle: the process of education versus the imparting of knowledge. While we accept innate differences between the two, through an anarchic approach we try to separate them on the one hand, while on the other we give them a chance to coexist. From this emerged another interesting direction, one that shouldn't be ignored – the integration into modern art development and our personal interests in the art of visionaries, folk creators, spiritualists, recluses, the 'mad' and the socially marginalised.

For as long as we have been collaborating with children – a very long period of time – we have learnt (and it has become a sort of ideology) that their different attitudes and abilities to represent emotion through the use of very simple abstract symbols in a very honest response, is the resultant form. For us this leads back to Malevich and Russian iconography – the source might be recognised as inspirational for Malevich and also as a return to the anarchism of Pavel Filonov, where the re-evaluation of self-directed elements evolved into an idea of form with a new significance – a phenomenon that Viktor Sklovsky described as an ability to make a familiar entity strange, to see the world in new ways, reconstructing objectives so that they are no longer understandable – a situation in which there are no restrictions. This is demonstrated, for example, in how Cubist painting intends to change our perception of everyday objects and forces the viewer to work in reconstructing the image.

Ultimately, we as tutors have found every experience to be a personal experience, each opinion a private opinion. We don't want to give any guidelines. For us everything that is written above is what we believe, our credo, our personal response, our individual understanding. ⌂

'Men in general judge by their eyes rather than by their hands; because everyone is in a position to watch, few are in a position to come close, touch you. Everyone sees what you appear to be, few experience what you really are.'
— Niccolò Machiavelli

Overview

The list is structured by professional architectural institutions. However, prior to reading and using the listing, it should be noted that the prime point of contact is the Union Internationale des Architectes (UIA), which compiles and periodically updates a very detailed and specific 'World List of Schools of Architecture'. This can be purchased via the UIA General Secretariat website. Alternatively, you can contact any of the other five primary key regions' unions, councils and associations listed here, which cover all matters architectural, and particularly education and schools.

For ease of use, the listing here also includes an extensive alphabetical list of the main institutional points of contact, country by country. Due to the huge number of architectural schools, these are listed under the professional architectural institutions of the country in which they are located, with a bias towards the institutions that give professional accreditation of architects. Where web pages are still under construction, readers are referred to the UIA website.

Choosing Your School

For prospective and current students of architecture, following is some unbiased guidance in making your choice of school. First, always plan ahead and leave no question unanswered. Research the Web for pages on the schools; if the pages have been produced professionally, you will find nearly all your answers on these sites – but don't stop there. Get other opinions, resource magazines, college catalogues such as end-of-year show pamphlets/ theoretical publications, books and, ofcourse, publications similar to this one.

Make a point of finding out about the dean, head of school, permanent and visiting professors, as well as teaching staff in general. Find out about their architectural opinions, work and theories. Research the courses and design/history+theory/ technology unit module work. Attend project crits, exhibitions, end-of-year shows and open lectures, and definitely take the time to consult with current and previous students, as well as always demanding an interview and a tour around the school. Ask about sponsorships, grants, funding and bursaries, as there may be options that enable you to attend a college you thought you couldn't afford. Finally, and most importantly, investigate the college's standing in terms of accreditation. But don't just accept the views of the accrediting bodies – for example, also ask the college itself.

UNIONS, COUNCILS & ASSOCIATIONS

Union Internationale des Architectes (UIA)
www.uia-architectes.org

The Architects' Council of Europe (CAE)
www.ace-cae.org
info@ace-cae.org

The Architects' Council of Central and Eastern Europe (ACCEE)
www.uar.ru

The Federation of Panamerican Association of Architects
page under construction

The Union of Architects of Asia (ARCASIA)
page under construction
hkiasec@hkia.org.hk

Union des Architectes d'Afrique (UAA)
page under construction

INSTITUTIONS

Andorra
Official College of Architects of Andorra (COAA)
www.coaa.ad
coaa@andorra.ad

Armenia
The Union of Architects of Armenia
page under construction
altida@netsys.am

Australia
Royal Australian Institute of Architects (RAIA)
www.architecture.com.au
national@raia.com.au

Azerbaijan
Union of Architects of Azerbaijan
page under construction
azer_architect@hotmail.com

Bahamas
Institute of Bahamian Architects
page under construction

Baltic Countries: Estonia, Latvia, Lithuania
Secretariat: Baltic Architects Unions Association
www.arhliit.ee/et/index.php
ealiit@online.ee

Bangladesh
Institute of Architects Bangladesh
www.citechco.net/iabnet
iab@bdonline.com

Belgium
Groupe Relations Internationales c/o Conseil National de l'Ordre des Architectes
www.OrdredesArchitectes.be
Conseil.National@OrdredesArchitectes.be

Bolivia
Colegio de Arquitectos de Bolivia
www.arquitectosbolivia.org/start.htm
cenacab@arquitectosbolivia.org

Bosnia and Herzegovina
Association of Architects of Bosnia and Herzegovina
page under construction
hamza.c@bih.net.ba

Brazil
Institute of Architects of Brazil (IAB)
www.iab.org.br
presidente@iab.org.br

Bulgaria
Union of Bulgarian Architects (UAB)
www.bulgarianarchitects.org/
www.bulgarianarchitects.org/
sab@bgnet.bg

Côte d'Ivoire
National Council of Architects of Côte d'Ivoire
page under construction

Cameroon
National Order of Architects of Cameroon (ONAC)
page under construction
Cab.Tog@camnet.cm

Canada
The Royal Architectural Institute of Canada (RAIC)
www.raic.org info@raic.org

Chile
College of Architects of Chile
www.coarq.com
central@coarq.com

Colombia
Colombian Society of Architects (SCA)
page under construction
sscanal@col1.telecom.com.co

Costa Rica
College of Architects of Costa Rica
www.colegiodearquitectoscostarica.com
coarqui@cfia.or.cr

Croatia
Association of Croatian Architects
www.d-a-z.hr
daz@zg.hinet.hr

Cyprus
The Cyprus Civil Engineers and Architects Association (CCEAA)
page under construction
cceaa@cytanet.com.cy

Czech Republic
Society of Czech Architects
www.cka.cc
cka@cka.cc

Dominican Republic
Colegio Dominicano de ingenieros, arquitectos y agrimensores
www.codia.org.do
codia@tricom.net

Ecuador
College of Architects of Ecuador (CAE)
page under construction
caesen@pi.pro.ec

Egypt
Society of Egyptian Architects (SEA)
page under construction
uiaegypt@mail.com

Fiji
Fiji Association of Architects
www.fijiarchitects.com
president@faafiji.com

France
UIA French Section (SFUIA)
www.architectes-fr.com/CIAF
CIAF@cnoa.com

Georgia
Union of Architects of Georgia
page under construction

Germany
Bundesarchitektenkammer - (BAK)
www.bundesarchitektenkammer.de
info@bak.de

Greece
Technical Chamber of Greece (TEE)
www.tee.gr
intrel@central.tee.gr

Honduras
Colegio de Arquitectos de Honduras (CAH)
www.e-cah.org
cah1@e-cah.org

Hong Kong
Institute of Architects of Hong Kong (HKIA)
www.hkia.net
hkiasec@hkia.org.hk

Hungary
Chamber and Association of Hungarian Architects
www.meszorg.hu
meszorg@axelero.hu

India
Indian Institute of Architects (IIA)
www.iia-india.org
iia@bom5.vsnl.net.in

Indonesia
Institute of Architects Indonesia (IAI)
page under construction
iai@ub.net.id

Ireland
Royal Institute of Architects of Ireland (RIAI)
www.riai.ie
info@riai.ie

Israel
Israel Association of United Architects (IAUA)
page under construction
architects@newmail.net

Italy
UIA Italian Section
www.archiworld.it
direzione.cna@archiworld.it

Jamaica
The Jamaican Institute of Architects
page under construction
jia@cwjamaica.com

Japan
Japan Institute of Architects (JIA)
www.jia.or.jp
myasuda@jia.or.jp

Kazakhstan
Union of Architects of Kazakhstan
page under construction

Kenya
Architectural Association of Kenya
page under construction
info@tectura.co.ke

Lebanon
Order of Architects and Engineers
www.ordre-ing-bey.org.lb
president@ordre-ing-bey.org.lb

Luxembourg
Order of Architects and Engineers (OAI)
www.oai.lu
OAI@pt.lu

Macau
Association of Architects of Macao
page under construction
macauaam@macau.ctm.net

Malaysia
Malaysian Institute of Architects (PAM)
page under construction
info@pam-my.org

Mali
Ordre des Architectes du Mali
page under construction
astec@malinet.ml

Malta
Chamber of Architects and Civil Engineers
page under construction
mfpb@maltanet.net.mt

Mauritius
The Mauritius Association of
Architects (MAA)
page under construction
mjs@bow.intnet.mu

Mexico
Federation of Colleges of Architects
of the Republic of Mexico (FCARM)
www.arquired.com.mx
info@fcarm.org

Mongolia
Union of Mongolian Architects
page under construction
uma_gc@magicnet.mn

Morocco
National Order of Architects
page under construction
cnoa@iam.net.ma

Namibia
Namibia Institute of Architects (NIA)
page under construction
nia@mweb.com.na

Nepal
The Society of Nepalese Architects (SONA)
www.sona.org.np
sona@htp.com.np

The Netherlands
Royal Institute of Dutch Architects (BNA)
www.bna.nl
bna@bna.nl

Netherlands Antilles
Society of Architects and Engineers
of Antilles
page under construction

New Zealand
New Zealand Institute
of Architects (NZIA)
www.nzia.co.nz
info@nzia.co.nz

Nicaragua
Nicaraguan Association of
Engineers and Architects
page under construction

Nigeria
Nigerian Institute of Architects (NIA)
nia@skannet.com
page under construction

**Nordic Countries: Denmark, Finland,
Iceland, Norway, Sweden.**
Secrétariat: The National Association
of Norwegian Architects (NAL)
www.mnal.no
nal@mnal.no

Pakistan
Institute of Architects Pakistan (IAP)
www.iap.com.pk
info@iap.com.pk

Palestine
Association of Architects in Palestina
(AAP)
page under construction
madar@hally.net

Panama
Panamanian Society of Architects and
Engineers
www.multired.com
spia_pma@cwpanama.net

**People's Democratic
Republic of Korea**
The Union of Architects
of the PDR of Korea
page under construction

People's Republic of China
The Architectural Society
of China (ASC)
www.cin.gov.cn
asc@mail.cin.gov.cn

Philippines
Union Architects of
the Philippines (UAP)
www.united-architects.org
secretariat@united-architects.org

Poland
Union of Polish Architects (SARP)
www.sarp.org.pl
sarp@sarp.org.pl

Portugal
Association of Portuguese
Architects (AAP)
www.ordemdosarquitectos.pt
RI@ordemdosarquitectos.pt

Puerto Rico
College of Architects of Puerto Rico
www.caappr.org
capr@coqui.net

Republic of Korea
The Federation of Institutes
of Korean Architects (FIKA)
www.kia.or.kr
fika2000@korea.com

Romania
Union of Architects of Romania (UAR)
uar.ong.ro
rna@com.pcnet.ro

Russia
Union of Architects of Russia (UAR)
www.uar.ru
narus@citylinc.ru

Siam
Association of Siamese
Architects (ASA)
www.asa.or.th www.asa.or.th
office@asa.or.th

Singapore
Singapore Institute of Architects (SIA)
www.sia.org.sg
info@sia.org.sg

Slovak Republic
Slovak Architects Society (SAS)
www.archinet.sk
sas@euroweb.sk

Slovenia
UIA Slovenian Section
page under construction

Socialist Republic of Vietnam
Association of Architects of Vietnam
hoiktsvn@hn.vnn.vn

South Africa
The South African Institute
of Architects (SAIA)
www.saia.org.za
admin@saia.org.za

Spain
Superior Council of Colleges
of Architects of Spain (CSCAE)
www.cscae.com
consejo.internacional@arquinex.es

Sri Lanka
Sri Lanka Institute of Architects
page under construction
sliasec@sltnet.lk

Suriname
Union of Architects of Suriname (UAS)
www.uas.sr.org
info@uas.sr.org

Switzerland
Swiss Conference of Architects (CSA)
www.architecturesrilanka.com
csa-archi@vtx.ch

Syria
Order of Syrian Architects
and Engineers (OSEA)
page under construction
osea@net.sy

Tanzania
The Architects Association
of Tanzania
joe@raha.com

Thailand
UIA Thai Section
www.asa.or.th/
office@asa.or.th

**The Former Yugoslav Republic
of Macedonia**
Association of Architects
of Macedonia (FYR)
page under construction
aam_skopje@yahoo.com

Trinidad & Tobago
Institute of Architects of
Trinidad and Tobago (TTIA)
www.ttiarch.com
chrismas@carib-link.com

Tunisia
Order of Architects of Tunisia (OAT)
page under construction
ordre.architectes@planet.tn

Turkey
Chamber of Architects of Turkey
www.mimarlarodasi.org.tr
mimarlarodasi@superonline.com

Uganda
The Uganda Institute of Architects
page under construction
ssenpart@imul.com

Ukraine
Union of Architects of Ukraine
page under construction
spilarch@amdemet.kiev.ua

United Kingdom
Royal Institute of
British Architects (RIBA)
www.riba.org
admin@inst.riba.org

Architects Registration Board (ARB)
www.arb.org.uk
info@arb.org.uk

United States of America
Association of Collegiate
Schools of Architecture (ACSA)
www.acsa-arch.org
aleal@acsa-arch.org

American Institute of Architects (AIA)
www2.aia.org
edelage@aia.org

Uruguay
Society of Architects of Uruguay (SAU)
www.sau.org.uy
presid@sau.org.uy

Uzbekistan
Uzbek Union of Architects
page under construction

Venezuela
College of Architects
of Venezuela (CAV)
page under construction
colegioarquitect@cantv.net

Yugoslavia
Union of Yugoslav Architects
page under construction
ep-arh@Eunet.yu

Charles Bessard passed with distinction at the Ecole Spéciale d'Architecture in Paris, under Paul Virilio, then studied at the Berlage Institute in the Netherlands. He currently works within Jean Nouvel's office.

Lindsay Bremner is chair of architecture at the University of the Witwatersrand in Johannesburg. She received her BArch from the University of Cape Town and an MArch from the University of the Witwatersrand, and completed a senior doctorate at the same university.

Michael Chadwick graduated from the University of East London after studying with Elia Zenghelis and Eleni Gigantes, then Pascal Schoning. He tutors, crits and lectures within both the UK and Europe.

Yung Ho Chang received a MArch from the University of California at Berkeley, became a licensed architect in the US, and has been practising in China under the office Atelier Feichang Jianzhu since 1993. He is head and professor of the Peking University Graduate Center of Architecture, and won the 2000 UNESCO Prize for the Promotion of the Arts.

Beatriz Colomina is professor of architecture and director of the Program in Media and Modernity at Princeton University. She is the author of Privacy and Publicity: Modern Architecture as Mass Media (1994) and the editor of Sexuality and Space (1992) and Architectureproduction (1988). She is currently completing a book on the relationships between war and Modern architecture.

Peter Cook is chair of the Bartlett School of Architecture, UCL. He graduated from the Architectural Association, and is cofounder of Archigram, a former director of the ICA, founder of Art-Net and life professor at the Staedelschule of Frankfurt, the UIA awarding him the Jean Tschumi Prize for all his activities. He was also winner of the Annie Spink Award for Excellence in Education and, most recently, the RIBA Gold Medal in Architecture.

David Dewar is professor of architecture, planning and geomatics and deputy dean of engineering and the built environment at the University of Cape Town. He lectures and consults internationally, particularly in southern and eastern Africa. He has been elected fellow of the university and a member of the Academy of Science of South Africa.

Eleni Gigantes was born in New Delhi, India, and educated at the Architectural Association before setting up Gigantes Zenghelis Architects. She has taught and lectured throughout the UK and extensively throughout Europe.

Christine Hawley is dean of the Bartlett and head of the faculty of the built environment at University College London. She was previously director of architecture at the Bartlett and lecturer at the Architectural Association, and is also head of the School of Architecture at the University of East London,

Tom Heneghan graduated and taught at the Architectural Association and established his office, The Architecture Factory, in Tokyo. He was been awarded the Gakkai Shoh – the most prestigious award of the Architectural Institute of Japan. He was also professor at Kogakuin University in Tokyo until he was appointed chair of architecture at the University of Sydney, Australia.

Jonathan Hill is an architect and architectural historian. He studied at the Architectural Association and the Bartlett School of Architecture, University College London, where he is now director of the MPhil/PhD in architectural design.

Vladislav and Liudmila Kirpichev were born in the USSR and educated at the Moscow School of Architecture. Vlad originally studied classical dancing with the Bolshoi Theatre. He won the

UNESCO Prize for the Centre of Public Activity project, and established the personal architectural school EDAS. Both have taught, lectured and exhibited throughout Europe and the US, based in Germany and London, and have reopened EDAS for postgraduate education in Moscow.

Iain Low convenes postgraduate programmes and research studies in architecture at the University of Cape Town. He studied at the University of Cape Town and the University of Pennsylvania, and was a Pew visiting scholar at the American Academy in Rome.

Peter Lynch graduated from the Irwin S Chanin School of Architecture of the Cooper Union, and is architect-in-residence and head of the graduate architecture department, Cranbrook Academy of Art, in the US. He is visiting professor at many schools of architecture, was chosen as an 'Emerging Voice' in US architecture by the Architectural League of New York, and in 2004 became a fellow at the American Academy in Rome.

Kevin Rhowbotham is a practitioner and diploma unit master at the Architectural Association. He has taught at South Bank, Westminster and the Bartlett UCL, and was also visiting professor at the University of Illinois at Chicago, and the TU, Berlin.

Neil Spiller is professor of architecture and digital theory, vice dean (academic affairs), director of the diploma/MArch (architecture) and diploma unit tutor at the Bartlett School of Architecture, UCL. He is also a practising architect, publisher and lecturer, and has exhibited extensively around the world.

Brett Steele directs the D[R]L Design Research Lab, an MArch graduate design programme, at the Architectural Association School of Architecture. He is also a partner of D[A]L, an architectural office in London. He has taught and lectured at schools in the US, Europe, Hong Kong, China and Japan.

Leon van Schaik studied at the Architectural Association and is the innovation professor of architecture at RMIT, from which base in Australia he has promoted local and international architectural culture through practice-based research.

Dalibor Vesely was born in Prague, and studied architecture, art history and philosophy in Prague, Munich and Paris. He currently teaches a diploma studio unit, codirects the MPhil course in history and philosophy of architecture at Cambridge University, and lectures throughout Europe and the US.

Anthony Vidler studied architecture and fine arts at Cambridge University. He taught at Princeton University School of Architecture from 1965 to 1993, then served as chair of the department of art history, UCLA, until 2001. He is currently dean of the Irwin S Chanin School of Architecture of the Cooper Union, New York.

Paul Virilio was previously emeritus professor at the Ecole Spéciale d'Architecture in Paris, chair and director of the same institution, editor of the Espace Critique collection at Editions Galilée, and was awarded the Grand Prix National de la Critique, before becoming programme director at the Collége International de Philosophie, headed by Jacques Derrida.

Mark Wigley is dean of the Graduate School of Architecture, Planning and Preservation at Columbia University, New York, and has taught and lectured at numerous other universities. He received a BArch and PhD from the University of Auckland.

Elia Zenghelis graduated from the Architectural Association. He has collaborated with OM Ungers/Peter Eisenman at the IAUS, New York, and founded OMA. He is now in partnership with Eleni Gigantes. He has taught and lectures internationally, and was previously professor at Dusseldorf Academy and ETH Zurich, based at architecture schools in Mendrisio and the Berlage Institute. He was inaugural winner of the Annie Spink Award for Excellence in Education.

Scenes from a Mall

The new Virgin Atlantic Clubhouse, an Upper
Class airport departures lounge in New York,
overlooks a retailing concourse reasonably
described as a shopping mall. Craig Kellogg
finds the lounge design, by Sharples Holden
Pasquarelli (SHoP), to be on a plane above
crass commercialism.

Below
The architects supplied a Miesian pavilion without walls, its steel-pipe columns half hidden by nonstructural slats of medium-density fibreboard. A neutral zone between the terminal's glass skin and the pavilion incorporates plain cube chairs to suit more conservative passengers.

It would seem an easy sell since North Americans love to shop and practically invented the indoor shopping mall. Following the latest model for airport design, a mall was built as part of John F Kennedy International Airport's new Terminal 4. There is a captive audience of travellers cooling their jets before boarding. (Due to security concerns, airlines recommend arriving as early as three hours before a scheduled departure.) But, at Terminal 4, the selection of shops and merchandise is as disappointing as the mall design, which features large metal topiaries entwined with artificial ivy.

Enter Virgin Atlantic Airways, the rock-and-roll carrier founded by Sir Richard Branson. In moving to Terminal 4, Virgin left behind a clubby VIP lounge near their old gates. For the highest tier of the airline's frequent travellers, as well as for Upper Class passengers (who sometimes pay 10 times as much for their seats), Virgin's new $2.3 million Clubhouse lounge offers an appealing alternative to spending time in the mall. Such expense was easily justified by the demise of Concorde; airlines are working hard to attract those high-flying passengers.

Because Virgin hires local architects in the cities where it builds, the Clubhouse commission went to New York firm Sharples Holden Pasquarelli. Virgin specified the number of seats required and requested a feeling of openness in the design. SHoP's solution brazenly overlooks the mall, with no walls to block the view. Indeed, those stranded in the mall's food court can see the Clubhouse floating above.

The view is a glowing advertisement for the Virgin brand. And that's how the majority of passengers experience the lounge. Access is strictly limited, so that in a typical day only about 225 customers filter through the space. Past the receptionist, a low burbling fountain helps mask any intrusive noises that might float upstairs from the mall. To one side, a few computers with Internet access are provided.

But the heart of the scheme is a Miesian pavilion with a gypsum-board roof painted white. The pavilion does not have walls or windows per se, yet still manages some sense of enclosure thanks to SHoP's system of perforated screens milled from medium-density fibreboard and finished with soft silvery paint.

During the day, the pavilion is silhouetted against large windows overlooking the airfield. But the slatted screens come into their own when artificial illumination takes over at night. Lensed spotlights on computer-controlled dimmers supply gradually increasing amounts of orange and red light as the sun sets outside. The effect was inspired by sunset bathing the office towers of Manhattan's skyline in a warm glow. A little extra sparkle is provided by Moooi's Light Shade Shade pendant-chandeliers that come complete with candle-flame bulbs hanging within smoky, silvery plastic tubes.

The furnishings, though obviously expensive, are hardworking first and foremost. The vast majority of Upper Class passengers simply need a place to sit. Complimentary food and drinks are served to visitors sitting tableside, semi-reclined or low and upright. For table service, SHoP supplied an endless line of café tables and red Saarinen chairs. Furniture by Eero Saarinen is a sentimental choice at JFK airport, where Saarinen's TWA terminal was completed in 1962 on an adjacent site.

Of course, 'some want a hard chair and a place for their laptop,' says Emma Lally, a senior designer at Virgin, and others 'want to rest their heads'. Simple cube chairs satisfy passengers with a conservative sense of style. Jeffrey Bernett's Tulipchairs for B&B Italia might suit anyone using a laptop, and his Metropolitan lounger, from the same manufacturer, has a headrest.

Top
Near the front entrance, a waterfall is underlit by submerged
diodes programmed to slowly change colour.

Bottom
Small café tables are furnished with Eero Saarinen's
mid-century dining chairs upholstered in red.

Seemingly at random, various brightly coloured
upholstery fabrics are distributed among the chairs.
The palette updates Alexander Girard's legendary
1960s terminal for Braniff Airlines at Love Field, now
only a memory. Alongside Girardesque fuchsia felt
and red bouclé, Virgin sports up-to-the-minute earth-
toned linen and coppery metallic leather.

But looking from Virgin's Clubhouse down to the
Terminal 4 mall and food court, it's easy to feel a little
nostalgia for Braniff, and more than a little sorry for the
current state of airport design. Airlines have lowered
expectations along with their fares, so that Virgin's new
lounge is not even as 'luxurious' as the one it replaced.
The mall has its artificial ivy, and now Virgin has a
simulated sunset. But even if Virgin does not offer
luxury in the traditional sense, it is certainly a step
up from the mall. What would Alexander Girard say?
A populist at heart, Girard knew that upholstery fabrics
in charming colours don't cost much more than drab
ones; he would have sharp words for the mall. Virgin's
standard-issue luxury offers a model for the
democratisation of design, even as it hovers just out
of reach for ordinary travellers. Δ+

Valentina Croci explains how architects 5+1 advocate a refreshing polemical pragmatism that is representative of a new generation of Italian architects. Having successfully devised a strategy for circumventing the conventionally closed competition system, 5+1 Architects has set out to work in a way that transcends the established practice model. Intent on using architecture 'to reshape an institution or function', the practice positions itself between the theoretical tail-chasing of academia and practising architects who so often regard themselves solely as providers of technical services.

5+1 Architects

Five penguins from the side, one from the front. This is the logo of Genoa-based 5+1 Architetti Associati: 'five' for the number of founding members (Paola Arbocò, Pierluigi Feltri, Alfonso Femìa, Gianluca Peluffo and Maurizio Vallino); 'one' for the cohesion of the whole, as well as for the approximately 30 people who collaborate with the firm at any one time. And 'penguins' because of their obstinate survival in the discouraging ecosystem of architectural practice in Italy. The firm's approach was different right from the beginning.

5+1 was established in 1995 by young graduates from the University of Genoa to discuss architecture and to work out strategies for dealing with the bureaucratic jungle of municipal administrations, who offer mainly episodic 'works' disconnected from organic development plans. The group also challenged the competition system in Italy, with its complicated procedures and highly individualistic approach on the part of

the participants. They began by looking to France, where some members of the firm already had experience. Ironically, their aim in 'going abroad' was not so much to reset their architectural culture as to seek design opportunities within Italy.

As a result, in 1997 the firm, together with Chaix & Morel of Paris, won a competition for the transformation of the former Bligny Barracks in Savona into a new campus for the University of Genoa. The firm also designed, with architect Rudy Ricciotti of Marsiglia, a public space in Genoa, and participated in the competition for the Congress Bridge in Rome (2000). By affiliating with such renowned firms, 5+1 has managed to circumvent the typical attitude of closure towards younger firms in these invitational competitions.

New University of Genoa campus, former Bligny Barracks, Savona, Italy (1997–)

The transformation of the former Bligny Barracks into the campus of the University of Genoa has been under way since 1997. 5+1 took part in the competition with the firm Chaix & Morel of Paris. In 2000, the firm's own project won the competition for the third and final phase – for the knowledge resource centre and the auditorium. The original barracks buildings date back to the 1920s. 5+1 sandwiched these between a brise-soleil roof structure and a wood platform in a solution that broke down the rigidity of the overall layout and rendered the individual buildings more permeable in several directions. The ambiguous territory defined by the brise-soleil and by the slender columns in fibre cement softens the boundaries between the interior and the exterior and offers a fragmented view of the sky, filtered through a sort of bar-code pattern. At the sides of some of the barracks, large full-height windows were opened up to create this exchange between interior and exterior. Projecting volumes (the architectural geometries protruding from the main building) and large spiral staircases below the brise-soleil work as service space.

Public Space and the Vulgar

Their collaborations with French architectural firms gave 5+1 an opportunity to compare notes and to exchange opinions. They approached the theme of public spaces from the point of view of the French landscape architects, weighing their theories against the many-faceted Italian context.

'This is a theme that has interested us since our university days,' comments the firm's Alfonso Femìa. 'It brings together the administration, inhabitants and resources of the city, an encounter with those who actually live in its spaces.

Therefore, we developed a design approach based more on the theory of doubt than on certainties.' Thus, neither design canons nor predetermined theories about typological and spatial composition, the firm's small, carefully designed projects are a rereading of urban layers and infrastructures, with special attention to negative spaces. If anything, there is reference to Giancarlo de Carlo's theories on the city and the territory.

'Firstly,' continues Femìa, 'an intervention in a public space should define the limits of the space and how it is to be perceived. In a Fellinian sense, even light and atmosphere become elements for understanding space. Elements that are part of everyday life in the city, such as the ugly, the banal, the vulgar, and our cynical relationship with traffic, are the materials to work with.'

An example of this is 5+1's Fornaci promenade in Savona, a walkway along the sea that is almost a kilometre long. The surrounding views are discontinuous and fragmentary, as is typical of so many of the areas of Italian cities built after the Second World War. The firm decided to shift the focus of the passers-by from the city towards the sea. They built a wall using rocks similar to those of the nearby jetties, in a distinct reference to the local identity. The promenade is separated from the roadway by bridges, urban furnishings and plantings that help restore a relationship with the sea. 5+1 dealt with the length of

Financial Police Building, Albenga, Italy (2000–03)

The Financial Police Building in Albenga is an example of an 'ordinary' building in one of the many mediocre townscapes in Italy that are never to be found on a postcard. The intervention substituted part of the existing building with a projecting volume and a canopy roof along the street. The canopy roof articulates the new facade and reorganises the spaces in the courtyard and the rear of the building in a functional manner. The projecting volume, which hosts the new meeting room, adds variation to the monotonous succession of buildings along the street. The use of colour is fundamental in this sense. While this is not a large commission, it is nevertheless an interesting example of the type of project Italian architects are most likely to work on. 5+1 has performed an 'ode to the ordinary and the anonymous', not in a cynical sense but in dialogue with the randomness of the building, in order to give identity to the space – without spending a fortune.

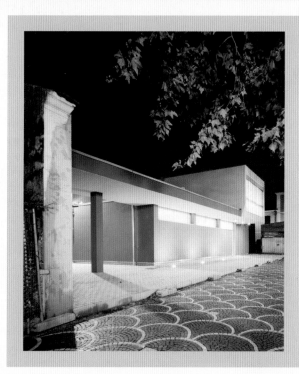

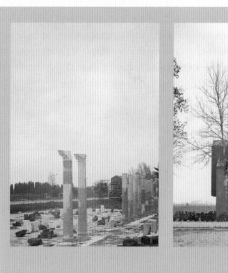

Museum visitor centre and antiquarium, Aquileia, Italy (1998–2000)

A series of walls in a basilica structure in reinforced concrete constituted the pre-existing building on which 5+1 based their project for the archaeological museum of Aquileia. The original layout was rearranged by means of three longitudinal 'grafts', using different materials and surface treatments: exposed bricks, plastered walls and fibre cement. The various materials were used on both the interior and exterior of the three structures. In terms of its relationship with the territory, the plastered portion, for example, looks onto the excavations. The building tackles the theme of historic layering on a three-dimensional level: the large window on the south facade faces the ancient macellum, while the safety stair along the entire west facade becomes an architectural promenade along the archaeological excavations. The indoor itineraries constantly refer back to the outside as they guide one through the museum. The project was built from 1998 through 2000, but interrupted due to lack of funds while the interiors were being installed – at just 200,000 euros from the finish line. This is Italy, after all!

5+1Architects5+1Architects5+1Architects5+1Architects5+1Architects5+1Architects5+1Architects5+1Architects5+1Architects5+1Architects5+1Architects5+1Architects5+1Architects5+1Architects5+1Architects5+1Architects5+1Architects5+1Archit
5+1Architects5+1Architects5+1Architects5+1Architects5+1Architects5+1Architects5+1Architects5+1Architects5+1Architects5+1Architects5+1Architects5+1Architects5+1Architects5+1Architects5+1Architects5+1Architects5+1Architects5+1Archit
Architects5+1Architects5+1Architects5+1Architects5+1Architects5+1Architects5+1Architects5+1Architects5+1Architects5+1Architects5+1Architects5+1Architects5+1Architects5+1Architects5+1Architects5+1Architects5+1Architects5+1Architect
cts5+1Architects5+1Architects5+1Architects5+1Architects5+1Architects5+1Architects5+1Architects5+1Architects5+1Architects5+1Architects5+1Architects5+1Architects5+1Architects5+1Architects5+1Architects5+1Architects5+1Arch
cts5+1Architects5+1Architects5+1Architects5+1Architects5+1Architects5+1Architects5+1Architects5+1Architects5+1Architects5+1Architects5+1Architects5+1Architects5+1Architects5+1Architects5+1Architects5+1Architects5+1Arc
chitects5+1Architects5+1Architects5+1Architects5+1Architects5+1Architects5+1Architects5+1Architects5+1Architects5+1Architects5+1Architects5+1Architects5+1Architects5+1Architects5+1Architects5+1Architects5+1Archite

Fornaci promenade, Savona, Italy (1996)

the interrelationships between the user and the context: the place becomes the central issue.

Yet there is always a synthesis between global and local, new technologies and the expressive values of tradition. 'Our only resource is the project. And the group with whom to discuss it,' explains Femìa. 'We are shaped by our itinerary: every competition or realisation is an important step in the growth of our architectural practice. Every project is a compromise. Every new opportunity is a test of what has been proposed.'

Young Italian firms tend to group together in order to get started, as is evident from the proliferation of logos in the last five years. It is a choice that allows the designers to supervise projects from the conceptual stage through their realisation. This is important, because it is precisely during the building stage that projects undergo the most testing. If the project is a design investigation, the competition is a means for conducting it. Once again, the group provides organisational efficiency, allowing intellectual resources to be applied to several different areas at a time.

In grouping together, in the absence of clear reference points, the members of 5+1 bring a sense of purpose to their design work. One day in Rome, 'in the shadow of' the statue of Giordano Bruno (a philosopher who, at the end of the 16th century, embraced the idea of reality as a plurality of signs that represent infinite manifestations of Being), 5+1 came to the following realisation. 'In the shadows of ideas there are no masters, nor fathers to stab in the back. We must move in the shadows, with force and determination. Designing rapidly is a necessary condition, because we are influenced only by the way things are. Taking a place in the shadows of ideas is a political position, not of resignation, but of combat. By exalting differences, shadows allow you see things as they really are.'[5] ⚼+

Notes
1 Sebastiano Brandolini (ed),
5+1: The Shadow of Ideas,
Skira Architecture Library
(Milan), 2001, p 119.
2 5+1, 'Aldo Aymonino', JA,
No 4, Josha Editore (Genoa),
2001, p 29.
3 Manfredo Tafuri, 'Storia,
conservazione, restauro',
Casabella, No 580, June
1991, p 26.
4 Piero Faraguna and
Tommaso Michieli (eds),
New Made in Italy, 8
architetture parallele, Opus
Editore (Venice), 2003.
5 Brandolini, op cit, p 119.

Valentina Croci is a freelance journalist. She has been part of the editorial staff of Ottagono, an Italian monthly on industrial design and architecture, for three years. She contributed to the first issue of the OP series of architectural monographs, on Santiago Calatrava. She graduated at the Venice Institute of Architecture (IUAV), achieved an MSc in architectural history from the Bartlett School of Architecture, and has recently been offered a place for the PhD in product and communication design at the IUAV. (Translation by Maureen Young)

5+1Architects5+1Architects5+1Architects5+1Architects5+1Architects5+1Architects5+1Architects5+1Architects5+1Architects5+1Architects5+1Architects5+1Architects5+1Architects5+1Architects5+1Architects5+1Architects5+1Architects5+1Archit
5+1Architects5+1Architects5+1Architects5+1Architects5+1Architects5+1Architects5+1Architects5+1Architects5+1Architects5+1Architects5+1Architects5+1Architects5+1Architects5+1Architects5+1Architects5+1Architects5+1Architects5+1Archit
5+1Architects5+1Architects5+1Architects5+1Architects5+1Architects5+1Architects5+1Architects5+1Architects5+1Architects5+1Architects5+1Architects5+1Architects5+1Architects5+1Architects5+1Architects5+1Architects5+1Architects5+1Archi
5+1Architects5+1Architects5+1Architects5+1Architects5+1Architects5+1Architects5+1Architects5+1Architects5+1Architects5+1Architects5+1Architects5+1Architects5+1Architects5+1Architects5+1Architects5+1Architects5+1Architects5+1Arch

5+1 Architects

Resumé

1995   5+1 Architetti Associati studio in Genoa founded by Paola Arbocò, Pierluigi Feltri, Alfonso Femìa, Gianluca Peluffo and Maurizio Vallino.

1996   First prize in national competition for the signalling system of Campi industrial park in Genoa.
Published Francia 2013-Italia 10. Non si uccide così l'architettura? – a comparison between French and Italian architectural competition systems.
Won competition for new hospital in Biella.
Seaside promenade of Fornaci in Savona.
Piazza Sant'Antonio and Viale Dante in Sestri Levante.

1997   Membership of the International Forum of Young Architects (IFYA).
Won competition for the conversion of the former Bligny Barracks into the new University of Genoa campus in Savona.

1998   Solo exhibition at the Italian Institute for Culture in Paris.
Public areas in the old dockyards of Genoa.
Won competition for the new archaeological centre in Aquileia.

1999   Biennale of Young Mediterranean Architects, Rome.
International competition for the expansion of the Law Courts in Siena – second phase.

2000   Exhibition at the Italian Institute for Culture in Prague and at the Venice Biennale.
Office building at Vado Ligure.
Financial Police Building in Albenga.
Competition for new Congress Bridge in Rome – second phase.

2001   Solo exhibition at the ETH, Zurich, and publication of the catalogue 5+1. The Shadow of Ideas
Solo exhibition at the SESV, Florence.
Mention for the International Borromini Prize – young architects section.
Won competition for the auditorium of the Accademia dei Lincei in Rome.

2002   Migliore Opera prize for Savona university campus.
Temporary pavilion for WylerVetta at the international fair of watches in Basilea.
Selected for 50 Nuova Architettura Italiana exhibition at the Hauser der Architektur in Graz.
Awarded Oderzo Architecture prize for archaeological centre in Aquileia.
Special mention in the third Hoesch Design Award.
Project for the former Magazzini Frigoriferi area in Milan – under construction.
Leisure centres in Moncalieri and Varese for Pirelli & C. Real Estate – under construction.
Master plan for Burgo area in Corsico, Milan – under construction.

2003   Migliore Opera prize for Financial Police Building in Albenga.
Refurbishment of King Ferdinando barracks in Rome – under construction.
Offices and classrooms of San Michele Museum in Cagliari – under construction.

2004   Knowledge research centre and auditorium of the Savona university campus.

Below
Proximity of railway to the site. The boundary of the site shields the
building from the adjacent railway and light industrial units to the south.

70–78 Rue Leblanc
Paris

As part of this ongoing series on contemporary housing from around
the world, **Bruce Stewart** profiles a scheme in Paris by Catherine Furet
Architects. Bounded by a railway line and a business park, 70–78 Rue
Leblanc is an ingenious exercise in space planning. Stewart describes
the merits and drawbacks of Furet's rigorous Corbusian approach.

Left
Transverse section through site. Since a basement could not be excavated
due to the steep railway embankment, the accommodation was raised a
level. Garaging is therefore on the ground level, with the housing units on
the levels above.

Right
Shared garden space between pavilions. It is hoped that the garden
spaces between the pavilions will bring the residents together and
create a sense of community.

Completed in 2003, the social housing at 70–78 Rue Leblanc,
Paris, in the city's 15th arrondissement, is part of Catherine
Furet Architects' long engagement with housing. Built on an
awkward brownfield site, there were many difficulties to
overcome with this scheme. However, the atelier never views
difficulties as problems but, simply, as challenges and
opportunities. Throughout her architectural career, Mme Furet
has held very strong Modernist beliefs in the value of space
and light and, in a very Corbusian manner, how an architecture
based on these principles can improve the everyday life of
the user. These Modernist concerns go beyond the simply
quotidian existence of the buildings. Integration into, and
the repair of, the urban fabric are also very much part of her
design philosophy.

Throughout her extensive 15-year engagement with
housing, Furet has continuously been in search of ways of
improving the quality or added value of her schemes. For
example, at Rue Leblanc, 51 off-street parking spaces were
required for 46 housing units. (Incidentally, Furet is anti-car,
so much so that she refuses to learn to drive, let alone own a
car.) France has very strict regulations regarding the provision
of car-parking spaces in relation to public housing, and one
of the most common solutions is to excavate a basement.
However, this can have large financial implications for what
are generally very tight budgets (see housing by BNR at
Montreuil in the previous issue). In terms of garage
construction, the normal spacing for the structural grid is 2.5
metres – and this is where architects fight for the residents.
They believe that such grid-spans do not provide enough
space to be comfortably inhabited by the residents above and,
therefore, recommend a grid spacing of 3 metres instead.
To accommodate this, the garaging is constructed as usual,
and large beams introduced to carry the wider-spaced grid
that will fulfil the spatial requirements of the atelier.

However, for the housing development at 70–78 Rue
Leblanc, the architects were forced to take a slightly different
approach. The site is a long, narrow strip of land that

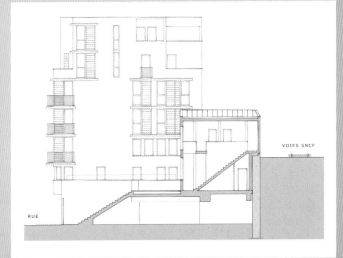

previously was largely a railway embankment.
Structurally this imposed several restrictions, not the
least of which was the inability to excavate a basement.
The solution was to remove the graded embankment
and erect large retaining walls. To provide the
regulatory car parking, the scheme was then raised a
level – garaging on the ground, accommodation above.

A further difficulty of the site was that not only is
the southern edge in immediate proximity to a railway
line, but on the other side of that a large business
warehouse development looms over the area. Here
the strategic planning decision was to split the housing
units into four pavilions that would maximise the
amount of natural light afforded each apartment.
This created the opportunity to provide shared garden
areas between each pavilion. And the splitting of the
accommodation into smaller blocks meant that four
individual family homes could be built in the resultant
gaps exposing the southern boundary. These houses
look out onto the gardens and protect the site from the
railway and the warehousing to the south. Breaking the
housing provision into pavilions works on several levels.

Top
View east along Rue Leblanc. By splitting the design of the housing units
into four pavilions, daylight into each apartment is maximised.

Bottom
Internal view of duplex apartment. The standard of the space planning and the
internal finishes to each apartment raises the scheme above the mundane.

Not only is light maximised and green space provided, but each block has its own entrance, giving the residents a greater sense of ownership and identity.

Entering from the street – via one of four locked gateways – there are two possible routes: either directly into one of the blocks or up a flight of stairs to the garden area and family house. The garden areas have the potential to create community spaces and bring the residents together, but there is also a risk that they will remain unclaimed and unloved. The range of accommodation in this development varies from the already mentioned individual houses to one-, two- and three-bedroom apartments, with the highest levels arranged as duplexes. All the accommodation is let by the HLM, a government agency that builds and manages public housing in France.

The architects have provided a good solution, in terms of strategic thinking and design decisions, for this difficult site. Internally the standard of the finishes and quality of the spaces are high, with an emphasis on providing social housing that goes beyond the merely mundane. The flats have plenty of natural light, and the larger constructional grid gives a real sense of space. However, due to the nature of the client, they are of a very traditional plan layout that does not challenge how people live their lives. The increasing numbers of those who work from home, and the fact that the traditional nuclear family is rapidly becoming obsolete, are not considered.

In terms of integrating the scheme as a whole into the urban fabric, the scheme is again a good solution, but again one that does not provoke or challenge. The immediate

The plan shows the long, narrow nature of the site.

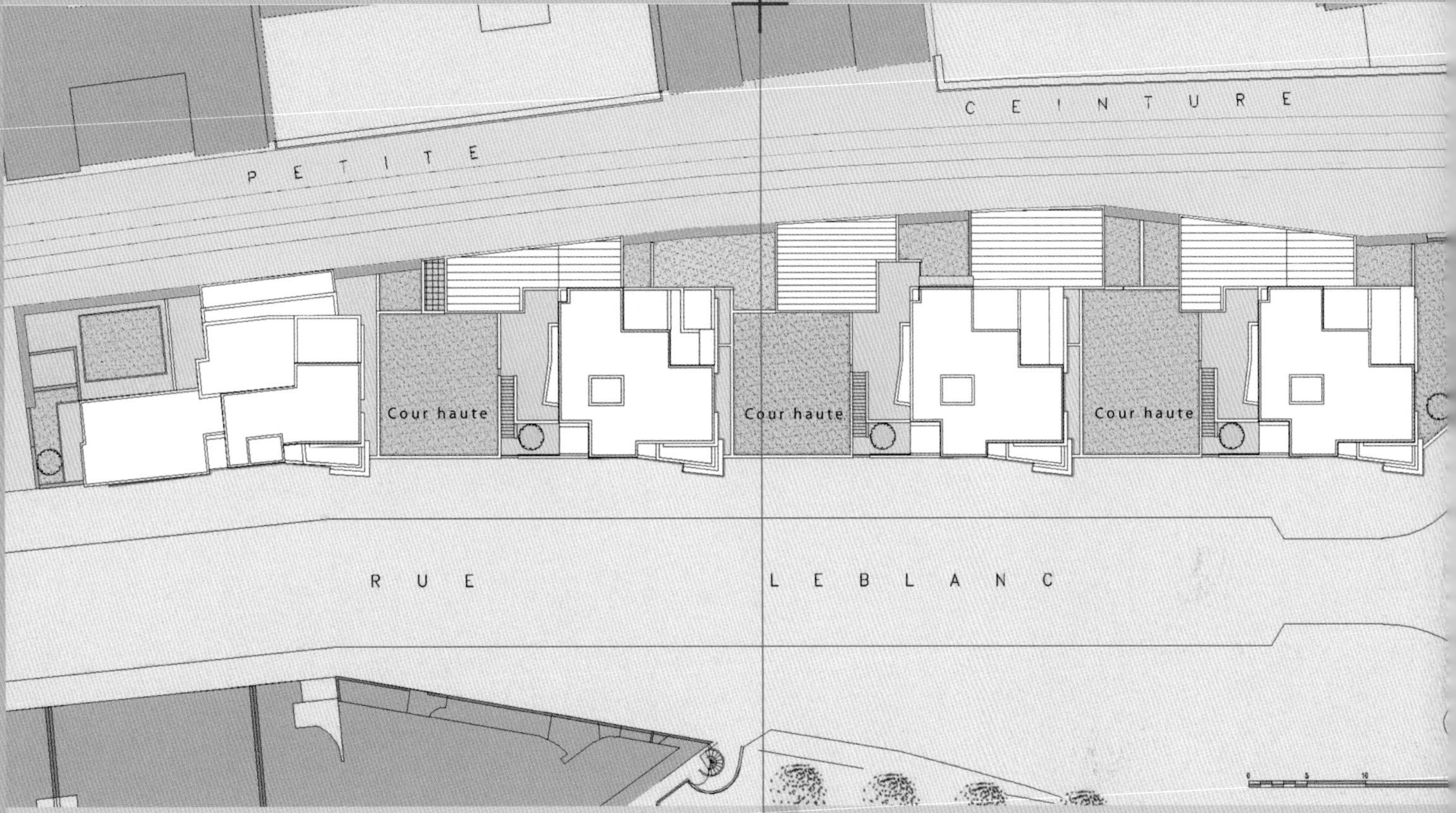

PETITE CEINTURE

Cour haute   Cour haute   Cour haute

RUE LEBLANC

RUE LEBLANC	G 0-29%	F 30-39%	E 40%	D 41-49%	C 50-59%	B 60-69%	A 70-100%
QUALITATIVE							
Space-Interior						B	
Space-Exterior					C		
Location					C		
Community					C		
QUANTITATIVE							
Construction Cost						B	
Cost-rental/purchase					C		
Cost in use				D			
Sustainability			E				
AESTHETICS							
Good Design?						B	
Appeal					C		
Innovative?					C		

This table is based on an analytical method of success in contributing to solution to housing need. The criteria are: Quality of life – does the project maintain or improve good basic standards? Quantative factors – has the budget achieved the best it can? Aesthetics – does the building work visually?

neighbourhood is undistinguished – to the west of the housing scheme is a large, Modernist-style hospital, and to the east, older, nondescript housing. The northwest corner opens up to the Parc André Citroën, which was created on the site of a large car factory during the 1990s. However, the scheme does balance out the large, white institutional architecture of the hospital and the lacklustre earlier

housing, while at the same time embracing the corner of the nearby park that it opens onto. Integration of the buildings into the wider urban fabric is a difficult issue to address in what has been, historically, a very industrial area of Paris, and while the scheme does acknowledge its neighbours it is a self-contained element in the wider streetscape. For example, the entrances to each of the pavilion blocks are discreet gateways within a long wall that do not completely engage the passer-by.

Critics of the work of Catherine Furet Architects may say that the practice's architectural language has an element of repetition, and that by adhering to Modernist traditions there is a stand-alone quality to the finished projects. Perhaps there is some truth in these remarks, but this is the continuing work of a very committed, confident and skilled design office with a real interest in the provision of quality spaces for the users. Despite the limitations of site and budget, the Rue Leblanc scheme does provide well-thought-through solutions and quality spaces in a design field known more for its compromise and mundanity. Δ+

Bruce Stewart is currently researching and writing, with Jane Briginshaw, The Architects' Navigation Guide to New Housing, to be published in autumn 2005 by Wiley-Academy. He trained as an architect and is a college teacher at the Bartlett School of Architecture, UCL, London.

Museo Picasso Malaga
Architects: Gluckman Mayner Architects, New York; Associate Architects:
Camara/Martin Delgado Arquitectos, Malaga; Engineering consultants:
Ove Arup & Partners SA, Madrid

Below
The new museum (white in the foreground with the main courtyard to the
right) takes its place in the historic though still working urban fabric, with
its amphitheatre, cathedral, working port and coastline that stretches to
the Costa del Sol.

Museo Picasso Malaga

Richard Gluckman made his reputation in New York in the late 1980s with pared-down
gritty gallery spaces, such as the Dia Center for the Arts. It was an architectural
treatment that was closely informed by Gluckman's own exposure to Minimalist artists
in the 1970s, but was transferred across to fashion retail and loft interiors and, with
the onset of Minimalism, came to be imitated Manhattan-wide. Jeremy Melvin explains
how today, some 15 years later, in Spain, Gluckman Mayner Architects is bringing into
play its extensive experience of museum and gallery spaces with the transformation
and extension of a 16th-century Malagan *palacio* into a new Picasso museum.

As the birthplace of Picasso, Malaga has something that its more glamorous Andalucian neighbours do not. A suitable celebration of the great painter might have made up in the cultural stakes for its Moorish fortifications not being a patch on Granada's Alhambra, and its Baroque cathedral looking stilted and formulaic alongside Seville's, but Picasso showed little affection for the city where he spent his first 10 years – especially after its Francoist city council turned down the offer he made to send a group of his paintings there. Had that come to fruition in the 1950s, Malaga would have had a powerful talisman against its status as capital of the Costa del Sol, where Spain's fourth-busiest airport spews out its cargo of underclad northern Europeans with anything but the complexities of 20th-century visual culture on their minds.

Fortunately, the old man's spurned generosity was not forgotten, neither in the city nor by his family. Once Spain's liberalisation had firmly taken hold – and the value of new art museums proved in Bilbao and elsewhere – the idea of a museum dedicated to his work resurfaced. Its prime mover was Carmen Gimenez, once an official in the Ministry of Culture, who helped lure the Guggenheim to the run-down Basque capital and is now first director of the Museo Picasso Malaga. Giminez reminded Picasso's daughter-in-law, Christine, and her son, Bernard, of his intentions and they responded enthusiastically with significant outright donations, and more on renewable 10-year loans – overall enough to give a sensible view of the 20th-century's greatest artistic chameleon. Armed with a major permanent collection,

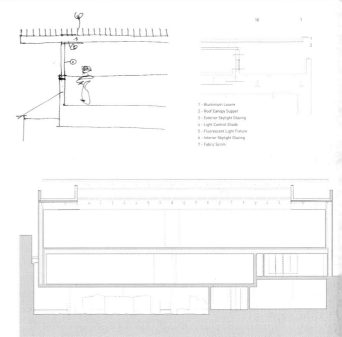

1 - Aluminium Louvre
2 - Roof Canopy Suppet
3 - Exterior Skylight Glazing
4 - Light Control Shade
5 - Fluorescent Light Fixture
6 - Interior Skylight Glazing
7 - Fabric Scrim

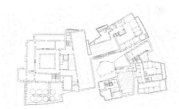

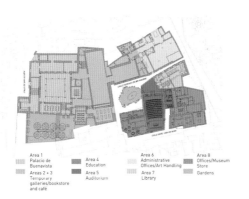

Area 1
Palacio de
Buenavista

Areas 2 + 3
Temporary
galleries/bookstore
and café

Area 4
Education

Area 5
Auditorium

Area 6
Administrative
Offices/Art Handling

Area 7
Library

Area 8
Offices/Museum
Store

Gardens

Giminez reasoned she could achieve something even more far-reaching than any amount of titanium crinkled according to the whim of aircraft-design computer programs.

Creating the new museum demanded architectural input of a different sort. It needed an architect who would not be frozen by Picasso's famous basilisk stare, almost as powerful in his work as it was in the flesh. It also required an ability to engage with the city, a robust port town where Roman amphitheatres and bullfighting rings compete with delicious courtyards and gardens to dominate the ground plan, while Counter-Reformation church pinnacles, Moorish crenellations, modern harbour gantries and surrounding hills vie for attention on the skyline. From its fabric and culture to its image in popular consciousness, Malaga is a series of disparities and contradictions: the birthplace of Picasso, who was contemptuous of it; an ancient city with a still working port; an airport known to lager louts across a continent, yet simultaneously a magnet for denizens of the Malaga Film Festival. And, as discoveries during the construction process revealed, the city had several surprises up its sleeve. The new museum needed an architect who could recognise the inherent complexity and necessary incompleteness of these dichotomous threads, not one who would impose a false unity on them.

At the beginning of 1998, having selected the centrally located Palacio Buenavista, from a list of three sites, because it offered the best relationship with the urban character, Giminez turned to Richard Gluckman of the

Top
The site section unites two and a half millennia of history, from Phoenician remains, to a Roman amphitheatre in the hillside, Moorish fortifications on top, and a cluster of Renaissance and post-Renaissance buildings up to the new buildings that form the museum.

Centre right
Permanent gallery on the upper level. Paintings like Picasso's Mother and Child (1921–2) on the end wall can demand total attention, though the architecture exudes a subtle spatial and tactile quality, whether it is the reminder of the courtyard through the windows (right), the opening to another gallery (left) or the restored artisanal ceiling and smooth new floor.

Bottom
The old door opens off the gently widening street to reveal an undogmatically new staircase leading to the reception desk (top of stairs, right) and courtyard (left).

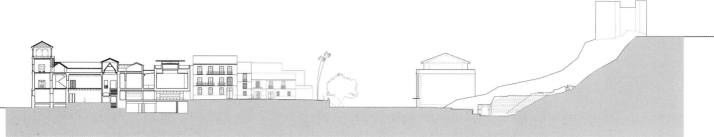

New York firm Gluckman Mayner Architects. His presence at hand was not entirely coincidental; he had already turned part of the local Bishop's Palace into an art gallery and produced a scheme for an art museum in Seville. Gluckman's reputation for designing settings and installations for demanding contemporary art is formidable, and in adapting Chelsea lofts to show installations by artists like Serra or Judd, he had often shown creative sensitivity in dealing with existing buildings. Above all he understood the subjective experience of creating, curating, exhibiting and viewing art: that each part is an essential and potentially endless phenomenon.

Gluckman's first reaction, remembers project architect Martin Marciano, was that the palacio itself would make a splendid gallery for the permanent collection, but that there would be no space for any further facilities. Giminez was keen to ensure that the museum should provide education, research and restoration facilities of international standard, and so initiated a process that saw the purchase of 15 further properties between the palacio and the Roman amphitheatre. Many were run-down and a few of historical value, leading to a subtle programme of urban infill, repair and reassembly of elements to constitute what is really a new urban quarter around the new institution. This alone is a significant achievement, but the design is a satisfyingly multitiered experience that belies easy definition or description, and whose complexities, surprises and variety resonate with Malaga's urban character.

Gluckman's initial perception became the starting point for the design. The rooms on two floors around an elegant courtyard house the permanent collection, while a new structure provides two floors of temporary exhibition space in a pair of T-shaped galleries. The distinction between new and old becomes a division between permanent and transitory, but that belies the design's subtlety and sensitivity to the act of viewing art.

At the main entrance the facade of the palacio pulls back slightly and its four-square tower creates a return to the building line, widening the street into what is not quite a piazza but is enough to arrest passers-by. The facade is cleaned but otherwise understated, though a generous staircase invites entry. It leads to the courtyard with the grace of a Saracenic garden rather than the didactic proportions of an Italian Renaissance cortile – a welcome relaxation. The first galleries open directly from the courtyard, but as the doors close the world becomes cool and internal. Here one can look at art, but

underlying the experience is a powerful architectural sensibility. One has been taken through several right angles, offering glimpses that hint at the rest of the building, and a dialogue between old and new has been established that might be preparation for the relationship between art and architecture.

In both instances, each component is necessary to offset its pair. The ceilings, for example, are fine examples of Moorish-inspired artisanal carpentry, while the floors are new polished stone. The most visible systems of environmental control are traditional grass mats hung in front of the windows; more sophisticated mechanical servicing is concealed in recesses. And the design seems intuitively to recognise that almost any of Picasso's paintings has the capacity to demand total attention, levelling every conscious sensation around it to an irritant or irrelevance. So Gluckman allows the spaces to glide almost imperceptibly into each other: at the point where Picasso becomes too much, an opening seems to appear, and moving through it seems natural.

Top
Curvature analysis of a portion of the roof is one of the tasks enabled by digital modelling of the building.

Middle
The roof's deflection under various loads – such as unbalanced snow load shown here – is evaluated using geometry data reconstructed from the equations specified by the architects and processed in a finite-element structural engineering computer program.

Bottom
Computer-aided analysis of light levels due to skylights proposed for the project can give both a 'false-colour' image mapping numerical values of light intensity as well as a more realistically rendered view, both of which are necessary in evaluating the design.

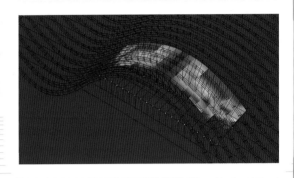

effort required for reworking and evaluating the variations. In order to put this into practice, the designers enlisted the aid of a Stuttgart architect, Arnold Walz, who is skilled in programmatic modelling. In this way they could generate the defining geometry, and all elements derivable from it, by means of scripting, that is, by programming the CAD model rather than creating it graphically.

Further refinement of the roof form then took place in response to factors such as egress distances, the ridge heights relative to each other, to the surroundings and to the building regulations, as well as structural considerations. This process made possible, for example, the elimination of interior supports that had been part of the earlier structural concept. In addition to aiding the structural analysis of the roof, transmission of digital files derived from the scripted CAD model also helped in engineering the facade, as well as in environmental studies such as those for evaluating the contribution of natural lighting and controlling heat gain. Although the CAD model was quite detailed, the architects continued to use physical models, too (for example, to study architectural detailing issues and the quality of lighting in the exhibition areas), and full-scale prototypes were also produced to test designs such as the roofing assembly and indirect lighting fixtures.

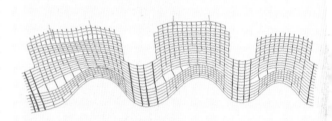

Following from the physical and CAD model studies, the roof structure was developed as a series of continuous, parabolic girders to be custom-made from steel plate, with intermediate bracing members made from standard sections. Subsequent to engineering of the steel structure by Arup, the architects' consultants, more detailed development of the geometry and connections was left – as is common practice – to the steel fabricators, in this case Zwahlen & Mayr, a Swiss firm with extensive bridge-building expertise. The fabricators elaborated the architectural and engineering drawings detailing the locations of key elements in the structure using other CAD software (specialised for metal fabrication) on the basis of the design team's setting-out data, which was transmitted to them in the form of tabulated coordinate points located at 0.05° intervals along the girders – generated automatically by the 'script'. The fabrication software was used to produce shop drawings describing, in detail, all of the steel components for checking by the design team and for use in the stages of fabrication that are not fully automated. Although the software was programmed to handle curved geometries as well as straight, close work between the fabricators and programmers was required to adapt it to elements curved in both plan and section simultaneously and keep within the required tolerances.

After approval of the shop drawings, cutting of steel-plate stock proceeded using a variety of machines. Elements to be made from standard hot-rolled sections (such as the braces between girders) could be cut to the required length from longer stock by a numerically controlled (NC) chop saw. The

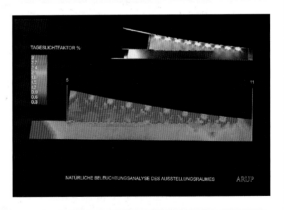

majority of pieces, however, were assembled from plates torch-cut from digital files describing the required profiles, for example for the webs and flanges of the girders. Markings for location of plate-girder elements at their joints, and of positioning jig pieces, were also made automatically with digital control. However, most welds were made by hand due to constraints such as the sizes and shapes of the pieces, as well as weld sequences needed to prevent distortion, precluding extensive use of robotic welding. Holes for bolted connections in standard pieces could be punched automatically by NC equipment programmed with the required hole sizes, patterns and locations. Accuracy of the finished girder sections was checked

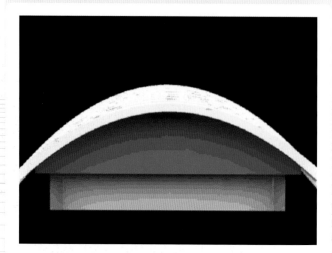

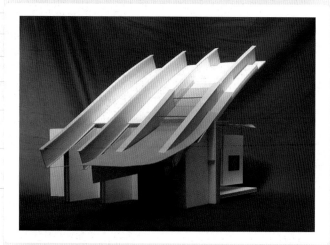

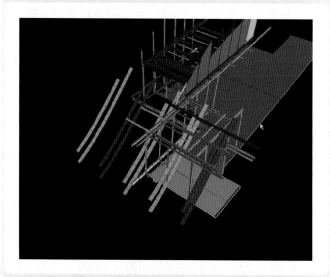

in the shop by conventional measuring processes – enabled by the circular geometry – and found to be better than specified due to both precise digital work and skilled manual work. Erection of the superstructure on site has proceeded largely without error, despite the complexities of its shape and details.

This project thus demonstrates the use of conventional CAD tools for both design and fabrication of a superficially simple, but underlyingly complex building structure, by extending standard software capabilities: through 'scripting' in the generation of the architectural digital model and through pushing the limits of the steel-detailing software by working with its developers. Definition of the complex roof geometry with sufficient precision to ensure its proper construction, yet with sufficient flexibility to allow evaluation of architectural- and engineering-motivated refinements of its form, required the use of CAD modelling well beyond the common practice of 'electronic drafting', an especially significant – yet quite natural – step for an architectural practice that does not ordinarily rely on CAD in any capacity but is acutely aware of the three-dimensional basis of its work.

We also see here, in tandem with digital techniques, the continued extensive role of physical study models and prototypes in an architectural practice accustomed to their use, allowing integration of the CAD studies into the firm's normal working process. Extension of digital techniques to aid the production of the physical models would further support the interests of a practice well-known for its concern with technical issues of construction. Ð+

André Chaszar is a contributing editor of Ð and a consulting engineer with an independent practice in New York. This article is the third in a series of case studies that illustrate the concepts and techniques of CAD/CAM in contemporary architecture, which were first introduced in the initial 'Blurring the Lines' series that appeared in the 2003 volume of Architectural Design. These and other texts are collected in a book of the same title to be published by Wiley-Academy in early 2005.

Below
The Genoese autostrada was begun in 1932, and was one of the world's earliest motorways. The road was completely rebuilt between the late 1950s and early 1960s, as were all the autostrada by the Intituto per la Ricostruzione Industriale as part of Italy's postwar Modernisation programme. The autostrada's many bridges and tunnels are the combined result of Genoa's location, squeezed between the sea and mountains, and the desire by Italian road engineers to minimise gradients and curve radii.

Architourist: Fiat Lux

On an improbable road trip across Europe to seek out the finest 1970s house interiors, architectural writer David Heathcote and photographer Sue Barr discover an enthusiasm for the autostrada that results in an unfashionable eulogy.

People rarely say they've travelled in Europe, partly
for fear of being mistaken for an illegal immigrant,
and because for most of us the journey is like some
nightmare suburban commute with the added risks
of lost baggage and deep-vein thrombosis.

Yet, travelling with only the most marginal sense
of destination is to experience a primitive sense of
freedom rooted deep in some rarely entered region of
consciousness. And travelling by car adds to this the
feeling of limitless possibilities that are only hinted at
by the redundant signs for Vladivostok that haunt the
commutered halls of Liverpool Street. To be sure, driving
anywhere is expensive, but abroad it is reassuringly
expensive. There the road is not some debased form of
infrastructural necessity running like a NIMBY sewer.
It is a celebration of going somewhere interesting across
somewhere beautiful, where you can stop, or not, as
you wish, and taste something new. But not only that,
in some places the road is an affirmation of culture and
civilisation, of sculpture and engineering and architecture.

In Britain it has been a long time since this has
been an acceptable discourse of the public realm, as
our roads are seldom any of these things (though 30
years ago the M5 was celebrated for its beauty in the
Sunday supplements). Last week, at the port of
Igoumenitsa, an appropriately liminal, marginal place,
we saw from the ferry the tollgates that marked the
entrance to the new road to Istanbul that stretched
upwards into the barren mountains, and felt the
pull of Asia beyond: not the pull of some beach a
tour-bus ride from the airport, but the whole continent
unfettered by itineraries of the grandtourette.

In truth there is the same promise at Calais, or at
Basle where you sense the Alps beyond and then
the lakes of Italy before its cities. The purpose of our
journey was to hunt down forgotten villas of the
1970s, but in many ways the biggest pleasure was the
architecture of Swiss transit and Italian autostrada.

On the outward journey we were just anxious to
get where we were going, and so rushed from traffic
jam to traffic jam on the major road. Yet on our return
we travelled in the spirit of paseo.

The autostrada from Florence to the sea,
Firenze–Mare, built in the time of the Duce, is as grim
and busy as the M25, relieved only by the idea that
somewhere nearby was the Church of the Autostrada.
It was raining, so we got off and went to Lucca to see the
early 16th-century Villa Torrigiani at Camigliano. There,
a decayed formal garden, the Giardino-Teatro di Flora,
was an essay in miniature of Baroque taste for the
counterpoint of formality and surprise. What at first
appeared to be simply a sunken walled garden was
in fact the entrance to an underworld of goddesses,
chiaroscuro views and watery grottoes.

The garden's tiny scale, and the heavy atmosphere of endless rain, created an exaggerated sense of dislocation, of moving from the rationality of the parterre to the irrationality of naked deities under the staircases. Perhaps this delight in contrast, of making the familiar strange and magical, is an Italian thing, because later that day the road along the Ligurian coast through Genoa made us rethink our limited English view of the pleasure possibilities of motorways. The autostrada here is fantastically bold, marching across the land oblivious of obstacles, a serpentine animal of concrete pushing beneath promontories and carried on slender legs over terraced farmland villages. As it reaches Genoa, the road strides right over the city past the upper storeys of tower blocks, past the container mountains of the port and over the factories, streets and old buildings of the suburbs. Contrary to northern expectations, this is not some nonplace experience; the speed, uninterrupted views and vertiginous traverses increase the sense of rurality, giving way to urbanity and industry and then country again. Seen from below, the autostrada is a sculpture, a monument to Genoese energy and ingenuity, as were the aqueducts to Rome.

Passing over Genoa, the whole country becomes a rhetorical essay in contrast to the sublime and the picturesque through the medium of the road. The autostrada is a macrocosm of the Giardino-Teatro di Flora for the common man. It allows us to stand above the world and admire its organisation. Its speed forces on us the contrast of civilised order and the rugged disorder of the hills, its tunnels, like grottoes, plunge us into darkness only to reveal new vistas where bridges become classical fragments, and buildings sculptures.

We headed north, and as we climbed towards the Alps the road seemed to shrink, no longer dominating but dominated, by nature. Beyond the lakes and Ticino, the roads lead to the high passes. Here, spectacular bridges and long curving ascents evoke a more adrenalised version of Turneresque Romanticism. Higher still, great concrete arcades sent us behind great cascades of turquoise ice towards hauntingly bleak plateaux and isolated granite Gasthauses.

In a plane you fly over all this stuff and know and experience none of it. By car you get the full grand tour, and with it access to the more visceral end of aesthetics delivered as much by the engineers as by the other culture you've come to find. Δ+

David Heathcote and Sue Barr are currently working on The 70s House in the Wiley-Academy's 'Interior Angles' series, scheduled for publication in early 2005. Heathcote's book Barbican: Penthouse Over the City, with photography by Sue Barr, is also now available from Wiley-Academy. David Heathcote is a design writer and historian. Sue Barr is a photographer and tutor at the Architectural Association in London. Widely published in the international architectural press, Barr has also extensively photographed authentic London café culture for London Caffs (author Edwin Heathcote), also from Wiley-Academy.

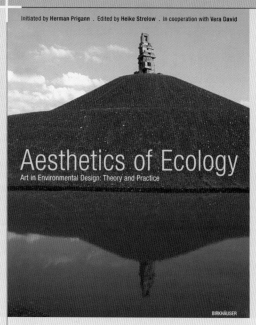

Aesthetics of Ecology:
Art in Environmental Design:
Theory and Practice
Edited by Heike Strelow
Hardback, 240 pages (200 colour)
Published by Birkhauser, April 2004

Reviewed by Brian Edwards

This book addresses the neglected cultural dimension to sustainable development by presenting a series of case studies and essays that explore the aesthetics of the ecology movement. In this sense, the book makes a valuable contribution to a debate that is normally dominated by rational scientific argument (for example, about global warming) or technological fixes (such as photovoltaic cells).

It is organised into three parts, each with half a dozen essays. The first, 'From Signs to Sculptural Places', presents largely phenomenological perspectives on art, ecology and symbolism. Although there is a fair sprinkling of terms from cultural theory, the essays are grounded in the real world of ecology and art. Nature, landscape and materials (from wood to ice, fire and water) form the backcloth to investigations of a largely theoretical nature. Key concerns like culture, poetry and perception are communicated through the medium of Land Art and installation.

The second part of the book deals with nature as sculpture and urban regeneration. Derelict sites (mainly in the USA and Germany) are used to show how the forces of ecology turn ugliness into beauty – aided by the artist who nurtures the process and the photographer who records it. What is interesting about the case studies is the role of design as well as art in the process of ecological transformation. The found memory, as Sharma would put it, is the beginning of artistic intervention. Derelict places, nature and art are brought together in an eco-aesthetic kind of way – that is, ecology portrayed as beauty, healing and sustainability.

The aesthetics of sustainability is a poorly understood concept, scarce in theoretical underpinning and rarely articulated through practice. What this book seeks is to develop a body of knowledge around green aesthetics. The argument is based upon the premise that society will more readily accept the discipline of ecological design if it is also beautiful. Not beautiful in the sense that artists make it so, but by the way artists and landscape designers portray nature in all its visual richness and spatial diversity.

The third part explores integrative landscape art. Although the word 'art' is frequently employed, the main thesis concerns the aesthetics of ecosystems. Art and ecology are discussed from the point of view of cultural politics in the hope of developing a constructive dialogue beneficial to both. Here the book strays into theories of public art, taking the art–ecology axis into squares and parks. The argument employed is that, since art is a form of knowledge, it needs to connect with the social, economic and technological worlds. Public art, inspired by nature, has the power to challenge the supremacy of other sociocultural orders. In this sense the book presents a compelling case to consider eco-aesthetics as a new style or movement in art. But the deeper significance lies in the power of nature to not just sustain life but to transform our cities, parks and landscape into places of beauty, or what the book calls 'forms of nature-friendly opulence'.

As a translation, some of the text is not easy to fathom. Yet in its simplicity of concept and the beauty of its production, the book promises to open up new avenues of artistic experiment. For the architect and designer, it brings the culture of cities and the culture of sustainability closer together. It suggests an approach to design that exploits the potential of eco-aesthetics to do more with less – to create more beauty from less intervention. To do, in fact, what nature does right in our backyard without the intervention of artists. △+

What this book seeks is to develop a body of knowledge around green aesthetics. The argument is based upon the premise that society will more readily accept the discipline of ecological design if it is also beautiful.

Bartlett Works
ARCHITECTURE BUILDINGS PROJECTS

Edited by Laura Allen, Iain Borden, Peter Cook and Rachel Stevenson

ex-Bartlett student who has ever practised from their front room – makes it intriguing sifting. It is organised alphabetically to ease the reader's keen scanning of inclusions, and each practice is colour coded at the top of the page. It takes in all the usual suspects close to the engine of the Bartlett machine: Cook and Fournier, Stephen Gage, Christine Hawley, Sixteen Makers, Neil Spiller ... And there are also those offices who have forged their most fundamental relationships through the Bartlett: Alford Hall Monaghan Morris (four out of four partners were at the school); Block Architecture (two out of two); Featherstone Associates (three out of three); and Softroom (two out of two).

Will Alsop may not be a Bartlett graduate, but there is a clear synchronicity between the energetic creative ambience of the Bartlett and the paint-splattering ideas lab of the Alsop studio, which might explain why it has proved such a magnet for Bartlett graduates. The short

Bartlett Works:
Architecture Building Projects
Edited by Laura Allen, Iain Borden,
Peter Cook and Rachel Stevenson
Published by August Projects Ltd
in association with the Bartlett
School of Architecture, UCL, 2004

Reviewed by Helen Castle

I have to own up to the fact that I have difficulty bringing myself to the point of even browsing many of the institutionally sponsored publications that land on my desk. The self-consciously overdesigned pages and tortuous texts have now only too regularly become a matter of course. Added to this is the sad fact that, however well-intentioned you are, it is impossible to raise your interest in a final-year project produced by a student from a college in Utah. My prejudices, however, were bucked by the arrival of the Works. I found myself taking it over to my production editor to discuss the format and the design. My colleague fully admired its wry and eye-catching cover image – a photograph of stacked boxes labelled 'fragile handle with care' – its lime-coloured tipped edges and rational readable structure (my censorious colleague had only one reservation – that the ppc matt cover was liable to tear, a prophecy fulfilled by my own copy). I took the book home.

In Bartlett Works, University College London's school of architecture has created an engaging hybrid: a catalogue of works by its alumni, faculty and associates which, like any project led by Peter Cook, maintains a joyous, vibrant quality and hence does not completely shy away from the 'where are they now?' human aspect. This, coupled with the fact that it is a selection – no attempt is made to be inclusive and take in every

In *Bartlett Works*, University College London's school of architecture has created an engaging hybrid: a catalogue of works by its alumni, faculty and associates which, like any project led by Peter Cook, maintains a joyous, vibrant quality and hence does not completely shy away from the 'where are they now?' human aspect.

introductory blurbs, presumably cajoled out of the office in question, are fascinating reading. Some practices volunteer personal and pertinent connections while many of the more sizable offices, who are recognised for their part as major employers, crisply churn out the usual praises for their own corporate successes – shame on them for delegating their contributions to their publicity departments!

The finesse and nous that Bartlett Works displays makes it an exceptional publication produced by a school of architecture. Its production and editorial qualities have no doubt benefited from Iain Borden's considerable experience of

publishing as an editor and author (Borden, who is director of the Bartlett, is a co-editor with Laura Allen, Peter Cook and Rachel Stevenson).

It is very evidently of the same stable as Borden's monograph of Alford Hall Monaghan Morris (they share publishers and graphic designers in common). Most cannily, the Works manages to be simultaneously an alluring tome and a knowing manifesto. At a time when even the most prestigious architecture schools are under pressure to justify their courses in vocational and technical terms, it sends out a very direct message

about the way that a Bartlett education can connect with practice by tracking the paths of its students into some of the most celebrated international offices. It is a very clear advancement on the view of the Bartlett as laid down by the Bartlett Book of Ideas in 2000.

I asked Borden why he felt that the school required a redefinition at this moment in time: 'We feel that the Bartlett School of Architecture has, throughout the 1990s and early 2000s, been pioneering a really distinctive approach to architectural education, asking our students and staff to be equally creative and rigorous in their design, writing,

'We feel that the Bartlett School of Architecture has, throughout the 1990s and early 2000s, been pioneering a really distinctive approach to architectural education, asking our students and staff to bea equally creative and rigorous in their design, writing, interpretive and analytic practices ... And often blurring these areas so that the worlds of theory and design, or history and technology, become truly integrated.'

interpretive and analytic practices ... And often blurring these areas so that the worlds of theory and design, or history and technology, become truly integrated. And in the world of education I think it is fair to say that our reputation in this area has become well-established. But it is also important to see how that kind of education might impact on the world beyond the university ... The book is both a record and a promotion of this activity.'

The book is certainly a most effective promotion as it maps existing relationships, highlighting what the Bartlett has done unsung for many years – engaging with international practices and supplying fodder to top firms. With a foreword by the Rt Hon Margaret Hodge, Minister of State, and a launch at Portcullis House as well as 'at home' at the Bartlett, the book has also communicated at a governmental and grass-roots level what it does best. The Bartlett, however, stands its ground, as Borden clarifies for me by describing the school's relationship to practice: 'An architecture school is not an architectural practice, and it is essential for a school to maintain its own sense of exploration, invention and analysis – one consistent with a university education that opens the minds of students (and staff) to new opportunities, creations and interpretations. On the other hand, it is equally essential for that same school to maintain a close and symbiotic relationship with the world of practice, benefiting massively from the extraordinary array of talent practising in a place like London.' This sends out an important message to other schools: to consolidate and remain true to themselves, while also being sure not to hide their light under a bushel. ⌂+

Le Corbusier and Women: the Naked Truth?

Abigail Grater reports on a new book that turns on its head the accepted opinion of Le Corbusier as a chauvinist, and shows the central role that his revolutionary attitudes to women and sexuality played in his work.

The work of Le Corbusier needs no introduction – one of the most influential architects in history, his creative output has been pored over by numerous writers. But an overwhelming prejudice has prevailed in critical writings to date: sexually voracious and fascinated by the female form, Le Corbusier has come to be seen as something of a misogynist, an objectifier of women. An authoritative new book is now being released that offers an alternative view.

In Le Corbusier: Architect and Feminist, Flora Samuel uncovers compelling evidence in Le Corbusier's personal correspondence, as well as in his published writings, artworks, architecture and urbanism, which indicate that his attitudes towards women were far more enlightened than has previously been supposed.

Part biography and part critique, the book examines first the impact of real women on Le Corbusier's life, and then the effect of his attitudes towards them, and towards gender and sexuality, on his oeuvre – with detailed analysis of a wide range of works.

Referring extensively to revealing and intimate letters, Samuel gives full accounts of Le Corbusier's personal and professional relationships with women. As might be expected,

RICK MATHER ARCHITECTS 113

Rick Mather Architects was founded in 1973. Its work spans both new build and renovation, with a special interest in the cultural and education sectors. Many of the projects form outdoor 'rooms' to extend both use and setting. As with my previous work at the Bartlett, John Lyall Architects and Gustafson Porter, at Rick Mather I have pursued an interest in balancing built form with themes of natural and cultivated public space – in the Virginia Museum of Fine Arts seen in the incorporation of the four-acre sculpture garden into the architecture.
Peter Culley

Virginia Museum of Fine Arts: expansion and sculpture garden, Richmond, Virginia, USA (with SMBW)
Museum renovation and expansion
Budget: $100 million (£60 million)
Completion: 2007
Peter Culley: project architect, associate in charge
The Virginia Museum of Fine Arts opened in Virginia's capital, Richmond, in 1936. Since then it has had major additions built in a variety of styles every 20 years or so. Our scheme removes the current entrance wing built in 1976 and replaces it with a large extension, opens up

significant areas of the existing building to public use, and replaces the current parking-lot at the centre of the site with a tilted sculpture garden with parking beneath. The extension houses galleries, the new main entrance, library, café and restaurant, shop, conservation department and offices. An atrium connecting the new and existing buildings has an all-glass roof supported by 600-millimetre cantilevered glass fins capable of resisting seismic loads.

A twelve-metre high by 22-metre wide window gives views out from the exhibition lounges onto the adjacent boulevard and over Richmond's downtown, reinforcing the message that this is a public gallery for all in a city which was racially segregated until the later part of the 20th century.

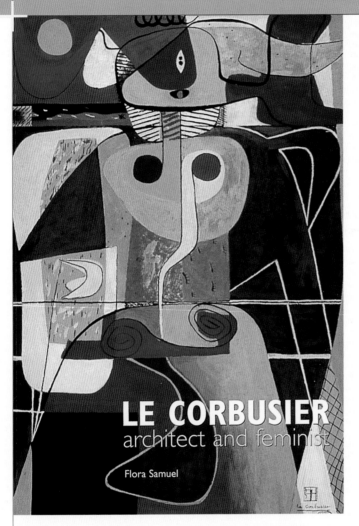

LE CORBUSIER
architect and feminist

Flora Samuel

the two most central women in his life were his mother and his wife; but his attitudes towards these two women are far from typical of a man of his time. He regarded his mother not only with deep affection but also with profound respect. Portraying her in a sketch, he depicts her not in terms of nurturing motherliness but instead as an awe-inspiring and wise sphinx. It was she who sowed the seeds of his enduring fascination with spirituality by encouraging him to look beyond the more widely accepted interpretations of religious and philosophical texts and form his own opinions. A musician by profession, she also had an understanding of Pythagorean harmony, which she likewise passed on to her son, in whose work it became a recurring theme. His sincere appreciation, throughout his life, of all that his mother had given him, is clearly evident in his correspondence with her.

Le Corbusier was similarly appreciative of his wife, Yvonne Gallis. A bold, spirited woman with a sharp wit, who shunned intellectual argument and enjoyed shocking the architect's associates with provocative comments, he wrote that she 'protected his soul from banality'. She became an icon, a muse. Samuel examines their relationship in depth, as well as those between the

architect and other women – clients, creative collaborators, friends and mistresses. It becomes clear that Le Corbusier saw women as potentially playing a key role in the establishment of a more harmonious world. Trapped by the structure and conventions of society, they arguably had more reason than men to seek social change.

Some of his attitudes may initially be interpreted as paternalistic, but closer examination reveals them to be based on respect. He supported the inclusion of women in professions such as architecture, believing them to be particularly well-placed to design housing – which, it should be stressed, he saw as the most fundamentally important form of building. He argued that housework should be seen as holding equal importance to professional employment, and advocated a five-hour working day for both the housewife's chores and the husband's business pursuits, the remainder of the day to be spent on the more important tasks of relaxing and developing relationships with other people and nature. Samuel records many anecdotes that endear Le Corbusier to the liberal-minded reader, showing his respect for women at every level of the social scale, from servant to princess. Photographs of him alone, and with women, show a rarely seen warm, relaxed side, in contrast to the familiar images of him as a suit-clad, heavily bespectacled, somewhat cold character.

Le Corbusier's respect for women was enriched by his adherence to Orphism and his investigation of related religions. He believed in the quest for harmonious unity – the balance of opposites, of male and female, both in life and love, and in the physical environment – and this became the most enduring central theme in his work. Samuel explains the main tenets of the philosophies he investigated, and the texts that influenced him most – from Plato to Pico della Mirandola, and from Rabelais to Schuré. She provides a wide-ranging account of the intellectual and spiritual climate of the Paris of Le Corbusier's day, setting his views in context and further underlining the ways in which his attitudes coincided with those of activists who were seeking the liberation of women.

This book is essential reading for anyone wishing to gain a true understanding of this complex and inspirational man, professional and private, and the driving forces behind his work. ⚙+

If you enjoyed reading this article, then you might be interested in purchasing Le Corbusier: Architect and Feminst, by Flora Samuel. 188 pages paperback (ISBN 0470847476), by visiting www.wileyeurope.com.

Subscribe Now

As an influential and prestigious architectural publication, *Architectural Design* has an almost unrivalled reputation worldwide. Published bimonthly, it successfully combines the currency and topicality of a newsstand journal with the editorial rigour and design qualities of a book. Consistently at the forefront of cultural thought and design since the 1960s, it has time and again proved provocative and inspirational – inspiring theoretical, creative and technological advances. Prominent in the 1980s for the part it played in Postmodernism and then in Deconstruction, ⌀ has recently taken a pioneering role in the technological revolution of the 1990s. With groundbreaking titles dealing with cyberspace and hypersurface architecture, it has pursued the conceptual and critical implications of high-end computer software and virtual realities. ⌀

⌀ Architectural Design

SUBSCRIPTION RATES 2004
Institutional Rate: UK £160
Personal Rate: UK £99
Discount Student* Rate: UK £70
OUTSIDE UK
Institutional Rate: US $240
Personal Rate: US $150
Student* Rate: US $105

*Proof of studentship will be required when placing an order. Prices reflect rates for a 2002 subscription and are subject to change without notice.

TO SUBSCRIBE
Phone your credit card order:
+44 (0)1243 843 828

Fax your credit card order to:
+44 (0)1243 770 432

Email your credit card order to:
cs-journals@wiley.co.uk

Post your credit card or cheque order to:
John Wiley & Sons Ltd.
Journals Administration Department
1 Oldlands Way
Bognor Regis
West Sussex PO22 9SA
UK

Please include your postal delivery address with your order.

All ⌀ volumes are available individually. To place an order please write to:
John Wiley & Sons Ltd
Customer Services
1 Oldlands Way
Bognor Regis
West Sussex PO22 9SA

Please quote the ISBN number of the issue(s) you are ordering.

⌀ is available to purchase on both a subscription basis and as individual volumes

○ I wish to subscribe to ⌀ Architectural Design at the **Institutional rate of £160.**

○ I wish to subscribe to ⌀ Architectural Design at the **Personal rate of £99.**

○ I wish to subscribe to ⌀ Architectural Design at the **Student rate of £70.**

○ ⌀ Architectural Design is available to individuals on either a calendar year or rolling annual basis; Institutional subscriptions are only available on a calendar year basis. Tick this box if you would like your Personal or Student subscription on a rolling annual basis.

○ Payment enclosed by Cheque/Money order/Drafts.

Value/Currency £/US$ [   ]

○ Please charge £/US$ [   ] to my credit card.
Account number:

[ ][ ][ ][ ][ ][ ][ ][ ][ ][ ][ ][ ][ ][ ][ ][ ]

Expiry date:

[ ][ ][ ][ ][ ][ ]

Card: Visa/Amex/Mastercard/Eurocard (delete as applicable)

Cardholder's signature [   ]

Cardholder's name [   ]

Address [   ]

[   ]

[   ] Post/Zip Code [   ]

Recipient's name [   ]

Address [   ]

[   ]

[   ] Post/Zip Code [   ]

I would like to buy the following issues at £22.50 each:

○ ⌀ 171 Back To School, Michael Chadwick

○ ⌀ 170 The Challenge of Suburbia, Ilka + Andreas Ruby

○ ⌀ 169 Emergence, Michael Hensel, Achim Menges + Michael Weinstock

○ ⌀ 168 Extreme Sites, Deborah Gans + Claire Weisz

○ ⌀ 167 Property Development, David Sokol

○ ⌀ 166 Club Culture, Eleanor Curtis

○ ⌀ 165 Urban Flashes Asia, Nicholas Boyarsky + Peter Lang

○ ⌀ 164 Home Front: New Developments in Housing, Lucy Bullivant

○ ⌀ 163 Art + Architecture, Ivan Margolius

○ ⌀ 162 Surface Consciousness, Mark Taylor

○ ⌀ 161 Off the Radar, Brian Carter + Annette LeCuyer

○ ⌀ 160 Food + Architecture, Karen A Franck

○ ⌀ 159 Versioning in Architecture, SHoP

○ ⌀ 158 Furniture + Architecture, Edwin Heathcote

○ ⌀ 157 Reflexive Architecture, Neil Spiller

○ ⌀ 156 Poetics in Architecture, Leon van Schaik

○ ⌀ 155 Contemporary Techniques in Architecture, Ali Rahim

○ ⌀ 154 Fame and Architecture, J. Chance and T. Schmiedeknecht

○ ⌀ 153 Looking Back in Envy, Jan Kaplicky

○ ⌀ 152 Green Architecture, Brian Edwards

○ ⌀ 151 New Babylonians, Iain Borden + Sandy McCreery

○ ⌀ 150 Architecture + Animation, Bob Fear

○ ⌀ 149 Young Blood, Neil Spiller

○ ⌀ 148 Fashion and Architecture, Martin Pawley

○ ⌀ 147 The Tragic in Architecture, Richard Patterson

○ ⌀ 146 The Transformable House, Jonathan Bell and Sally Godwin